Previously published: **PUBLIC AFFAIRS AND POWER**
ESSAYS IN A TIME OF FEAR
(Landmarks Publishing)

EVERYTHING FLOWS
ESSAYS ON PUBLIC AFFAIRS AND CHANGE
(Landmarks Publishing)

CHALLENGE & RESPONSE
ESSAYS ON PUBLIC AFFAIRS & TRANSPARENCY
(Landmarks Publishing)

THE FUTURE OF PUBLIC TRUST
PUBLIC AFFAIRS IN A TIME OF CRISIS

Edited by Tom Spencer and Conor McGrath

DODS Published in association with
the European Centre for Public Affairs

Cover photography: Joe Gough/Shutterstock

The views expressed are those of the authors
and do not represent the position of Dods or
the European Centre for Public Affairs.

All rights reserved. No reproduction,
copy or transmission of this publication
can be made without written permission.

© ECPA 2008

First published in 2008
by Dods
Westminster Tower
3 Albert Embankment
London SE1 7SP
www.dodonline.co.uk

ISBN 978-0-905702-84-1

Printed and bound in Belgium on certified FSC (Forest Stewardship Council) paper.

Dedicated to the Unknown Lobbyist ...

Contents

FOREWORD *Roland Verstappen, Chairman ECPA Management Board* 8
PREFACE The Opportunity for Public Affairs
          Tom Spencer and Conor McGrath 10

Part I. TRANSPARENCY: THE CONTINUING STORY
        OF AN INITIATIVE 13
  1. Integrity and Trust *Erik Jonnaert* 13
  2. The European Transparency Initiative: A Ring Cycle for Today?
     Tom Spencer 17
  3. Lobbying and the ETI: Irony and Instruction *Steven Billet* 21
  4. The Context and Inspiration of the European Transparency
     Initiative *Kristian Schmidt* 29
  5. The Continuing ETI Process: The Genesis, Functioning and
     Future of the Commission's Register for Interest Representatives
     Jens Nymand Christensen 35
  6. A Framework for Lobbyists in the European Institutions
     Ingo Friedrich MEP 41
  7. Transparency and the European Ombudsman
     P. Nikiforos Diamandouros 45
  8. Building Trust with the EU Citizen: Is Anyone Listening?
     José Lalloum 53
  9. The European Transparency Initiative – Barking Up the Wrong Tree?
     Irina Michalowitz 57
  10. Registering Intelligently?: An ECPA Recommendation
      Conor McGrath 67

Part II. PUBLIC AFFAIRS BEST PRACTICE 73
1. Hiring Public Affairs Consultants *Summary of Recommendations from an ECPA Working Group* 73
2. Trade Associations and Their Corporate Members *Summary of Recommendations from an ECPA Working Group* 79
3. German and Austrian Public Affairs *Irina Michalowitz and Peter Köppl* 85
4. Public Affairs in Europe – The Same Everywhere or Different? *Michael Burrell* 95
5. Social Media – An Unmissable Opportunity for Public Affairs? *Amber Price* 105

Part III. POLITICS AND PUBLIC AFFAIRS 111
1. Of Rogues, Bishops and Golden Toads *Tom Spencer* 111
2. A Novel Look at Lobbyists *Conor McGrath* 117
3. The Public Affairs of Sunshine *Tom Spencer* 125
4. First Things, Last Things: The Public Affairs of Priorities *Tom Spencer* 131
5. Beyond Black & White – The Public Affairs of Global Crises *Tom Spencer* 137

Part IV. AUTHORS' BIOGRAPHIES 145

Foreword

Dear Reader,

I am delighted, as Chairman of the Management Board of the European Centre for Public Affairs, to introduce you to this fourth book of essays from my friends and colleagues at the ECPA. For many years, first with Ford of Europe and now with ArcelorMittal, I have participated in and enjoyed the debates, seminars and conferences of the ECPA. I know of no other space where practitioners and academics co-operate so comfortably and creatively in search of wisdom in the world of public affairs.

These essays reflect the work of the Centre in the last two years. I am particularly grateful to busy practitioner colleagues who have made the time to invest in the future of public affairs by putting their thoughts on paper.

The ECPA has been publicly active in the continuing story of the European Transparency Initiative in the last twelve months. This follows the decision by my predecessor as Chairman, Erik Jonnaert, to bring together the ECPA, SEAP and EPACA to pool our resources in the debate about lobbying. All three organisations share a desire to promote public affairs best practice, as symbolised by our endorsement of the new EPAD European Public Affairs Awards. However we are all aware of the damage that can be done to the credibility of the public affairs process by ignorant criticism or ill thought out political initiatives.

I chaired the ECPA Management Board Seminar on 9 October 2008 when we hosted a discussion involving some 40 organisations. The participants were made up of the traditional ECPA mix of in-house practitioners, consultants, NGOs and trade association executives. I find it interesting that every public affairs organisation represented at the meeting was happy to register voluntarily under the ETI in a spirit of co-operation, even if we all have suggestions as to how the process might be improved, rendered more coherent and preferably extended to all European institutions. However I know that I speak for everyone involved in the ECPA when I stress that Registers and Codes are only a means to an end.

Foreword

As Erik Jonnaert says in the first essay in this book, "Those of us active in public affairs or public relations know that integrity and trust are key building blocks for our profession". It is the quality of public trust in the political process, of which public affairs forms part, that has come under increasing threat in recent years on both sides of the Atlantic. Now, in a full-blown financial and systemic crisis, we need to devote even more time to explaining what public affairs is about and to winning back the public trust that has been undermined by the action of certain individuals.

Catherine Stewart, in reviewing an earlier book of ECPA essays, commended the format as suitable for the lifestyle of a busy public affairs practitioner. "Each essay is the right length to be enjoyed while waiting to board an aircraft," she claimed. There is humour as well as learning in these pages, so I am happy to commend the volume to you, whether you are reading it in a university library or a departure lounge.

Roland Verstappen
Chairman, ECPA Management Board
Vice President, International Affairs, ArcelorMittal

Preface

The Opportunity for Public Affairs

We are pleased to introduce this collection on essays on the opportunity for public affairs which is presented by the debate about the regulation of lobbyists and the current period of global crisis. This is the fourth volume in a series designed to make available the perspectives of professionals, academics and officials at a reasonable price. Our thanks go to our contributors and our publisher for having made the process of producing this text so enjoyable. While not responsible for any statements of fact or opinion by the contributors, the European Centre for Public Affairs is delighted to offer them this platform to present their views. It is our hope that the book can help to stimulate discussion and debate among all those who share our interest in high standards and ethical conduct.

Recent years have seen a decline in "public trust" in politics. Many had come to believe that neither politicians nor public affairs practitioners could ever again inspire confidence. The election of President Obama is a clear indication that electorates are still prepared to trust leaders who they think capable of facing the challenges of a paradigm shift in human affairs. For practitioners to achieve a similar confidence requires that they constantly strive for the "best practice in public affairs" which has been at the heart of the work undertaken by the European Centre for Public Affairs since its foundation in 1988.

There has been much talk of how an Obama Administration will have different relations with lobbyists. There will be some adjustments – Obama refused to accept campaign contributions from lobbyists, and has pledged that lobbyists will not be given positions in his administration in which they would have responsibility for their former industries. Equally, though, Obama has a full policy programme which will inevitably bring with it extensive legislative lobbying opportunities. It is doubtful that the American system is about to change fundamentally. However in both America and Europe we are likely to see continued demands for greater transparency and accountability in the practice of public affairs. We should not regard this as a threat, rather we should see it as an opportunity for public affairs. An opportunity to show that the practice of public affairs in a time of crisis is about the serious defence of reputation rather than an exercise in transient spin. In recent years we have seen huge companies and organisations disappear overnight. Public affairs practitioners who want to avoid that fate for their organisations will need to base their external communications on a clear base of internal realities and internal communications. In a time of political and economic upheaval such as this, the public affairs function becomes even more important. Navigating the complexity and uncertainty of change requires that organisations can draw upon experience and expertise in public affairs. New agendas bring a need for an understanding of personalities, policy and process. Effective dealings with government and society are now more crucial than ever to overall success. The key to positive engagement today is leadership. Public affairs practitioners need to be influential not just in the public policy arena but within their own organisation. PA has always been an important management function, but increasingly it has to be central to the engine room of any organisation. It must be highly visible to every other internal unit; it must demonstrate its contribution and relevance across all parts of the business.

At a collective level, lobbyists recognise that issues of accountability and transparency can no longer be addressed through a discussion among the political elite. There is a clear public interest involved here. Lobbying is central to democracy; an interest group system is – alongside parties, elections, parliaments, executives and bureaucracies – core to the workings of a free political system. But with this comes a professional responsibility to ensure appropriate standards of conduct and to be seen to be acting ethically. There is also an opportunity here for leadership and renewal on the part of those bodies which represent public affairs practitioners, ECPA included. We have a role to play in bringing together professionals; helping to train, educate and motivate them; defending their interests and values to policy-makers; and offering more proactive and vigorous direction to efforts to inform the public about the legitimate role of lobbying.

The debate about the European Transparency Initiative is at an interesting point. The SEAP conference on 5 November 2008 revealed an emerging consensus among practitioners about the way ahead. Such a consensus will be helped by two trends. The departure of Commissioner Kallas provides the opportunity to take a new look at the issue. The learning experience of filling in the voluntary register is already beginning to culture a consensus amongst experienced practitioners that they could live with light touch regulation.

The next twelve months will be a period of consolidation and creativity. Those of us involved in the struggle to create a robust but realistic framework for the conduct of public affairs should draw some inspiration from the conduct of the Obama campaign – stay on message, stay calm, take all available opportunities.

Tom Spencer and Conor McGrath
16 November 2008

Part I. TRANSPARENCY: THE CONTINUING STORY OF AN INITIATIVE

1. *Integrity and Trust*
Erik Jonnaert

Let me be clear from the start: I have no objections against the current proposals on the table for more transparency for lobbying in Brussels and for promoting ethical behaviour for public affairs professionals. As chairman of ECPA, I have always taken the point of view that a code or registration system can only help if it is a means to an end and not an end in itself.

Those of us active in public affairs or public relations know that integrity and trust are key building blocks for our profession. These go beyond a registration system or code.

Integrity and trust are key if we want to succeed in our mission as PA or PR professionals, which is all about managing and shaping the communication between the organisation to which we belong or which we represent and its target audiences in order to build, manage and sustain a positive reputation. For those of us who play a more focused role in public affairs or government relations, our mission is all about managing, shaping and leveraging policy and legislation in a balanced way and correctly reflecting the point of view of either the organisation to which we belong or which we represent.

Ivy Lee, who lived in the US from 1877 to 1934 and who is considered as one of the founders of modern public relations, supported in the beginning of the last century a philosophy for PR, consistent with what has sometimes been called the "two way street" approach to PR and PA, in which PR consists of helping clients listen as well as communicate messages to their public. He articulated the concept that PR practitioners have a public responsibility that extends beyond obligations to their client.

In a way, PA and PR practitioners are like ambassadors for their organisations or clients. They communicate externally the point of view of the organisation they represent but also translate back into the organisation the point of view of others. In PR and PA, integrity and trust are key to moving forward. Let me add some perspective on integrity and trust as building blocks for our profession.

Many look at integrity and ethics as one and the same. I disagree. Ethics debates like the one we have today on lobbyists are focusing on compliance. It is about following rules, not on clarifying values and fostering integrity to those values and principles.

As Albert Camus stated: integrity has no need of rules. Integrity is about honesty, but it is also about congruence or harmony, humility and courage:

- People are congruent when they act in harmony with their deepest values and beliefs, when there's no gap between intent and behaviour. Scandals we often hear about are often about either mismatch between values and behaviour or about complete absence of values in the first place.
- People should be humble by being more concerned about what's right than about being right, about acting on good ideas than having the ideas. Humble people realize they do not act alone (never) but always build upon what others have already accomplished.
- People should be courageous to speak up to ensure they do the right things and do not accept to engage in unethical behaviour. This means for PA practitioners standing up against their organisation if needed and for consultants against their clients if requested to do what does not seem right.

PA and PR practitioners should be honest, should act in a way which is in line with what they believe in, should do this in a modest and humble way while standing up and going against the tide if this is what needs to be done. If we have not fixed that first, I am afraid that no code or registration system will help moving us forward.

Next to integrity, I would add trust as the next key building block for PA and PR practitioners. Let me add that trust is key for all people in life. If the European Union today has a bit of a problem with its citizens, it is because of the trust gap. Once there is a trust gap, everything slows down.

I got very much inspired by Stephen Covey's latest book on *The Speed of Trust*, where he argues that low trust causes friction, low trust is the greatest cost in life and in organisations, including families. Low trust slows down every decision, every communication, every relationship. On the other hand, trust produces speed. When people trust each other, when organisations trust each other, we can deliver together great results, faster.

When there's lack of trust, we see interventions to fix the trust gap, often through legislation, rules, restrictions. Because of these interventions, things are getting slower ... we then feel we need to build trust by complying with rules first – which often takes time and is cumbersome. Stephen Covey calls this the trust tax we pay.

Recent research like that done by Edelman through their trust barometer demonstrated how big the gaps are in trust between society at large and its economic and social actors.

Last year's trust barometer issued by Edelman even showed that trust in government and media is low and going lower in both the US and the EU while trust in business is growing. NGOs are now the most trusted institutions in nearly every market in the world. In Europe, top in the league would be NGOs, followed by business, followed by government and the media ending up in 4th place. This trend was confirmed for Western Europe – in France, Germany, Italy, Spain and the UK – except for France where trust in government is higher than in business. An interesting insight from the research was that trust in institutions/organisations in Europe is lower than any other market in the world. This partly explains the identity crisis of the European Union.

So, how to build and maintain trust? Again, a code or registration system may help but will not be the solution to the trust challenge. As Steven Covey puts it: trust is a function of both character and competence. Character includes integrity, which I just talked about. Competence includes your skills, your results, your track record. People trust people who make things happen.

The increasing concern about ethics has been good for our society – is good for PA and PR in Europe. Ethics is foundational to trust but not enough. You can't have trust without ethics but you can have ethics without trust.

Trust which includes ethics is the bigger idea. Trust is about character and competence – it's about heart and head in what we do and how we do it.

Driving competence among PA practitioners has been the core business of our European Centre for Public Affairs: focusing on identifying and exchanging best practices within the profession.

Let's actively engage in the debate initiated by Commissioner Kallas on transparency and ethics in lobbying. At the same time, I would encourage each of us not to forget the fundamentals in our profession: integrity and trust.

Originally written as a speech delivered at the inauguration of Philip Sheppard as president of the International Public Relations Association in January 2007.

2. The European Transparency Initiative: A Ring Cycle for Today?

Tom Spencer

Public affairs, the interaction of society with its political institutions, is serious stuff. It is essential to democracy, particularly to a "new" democracy on a continental scale. The examples of the USA and India should remind us that such democracies are possible, even as they warn us of dangers ahead.

It is truly tragic therefore that the debate about the European Transparency Initiative, as it relates to public affairs, has never risen above the level of soap opera. For four years we have been treated to regular instalments of the superficial, driven by personality and sliced into 90-second sound bites. It is as if the Ring Cycle had been written by Wikipedia rather than Wagner. Great themes, but no linking leitmotif. Great characters, but no direction and no evolution. Diatribe not dialogue.

The plot so far does not reflect well on any of the performers. The public affairs culture of the European Union is in transition, but it is not broken. The question of lobbying was included in the European Transparency Initiative, and is maintained in the public eye, by a brilliant but ruthless campaign directed by the Corporate Europe Observatory. The role of Albrecht is taken convincingly by Erik Wesselius, who on behalf of Nibelungen everywhere, passionately believes that public affairs is the ring of power, which if possessed can break the hold of capitalism on the European Union. Campaigners in the grip of such certainty see nothing immoral in personal viciousness, trial by website or in stooping to the worst supposed habits of the very system which they seek to overthrow. The campaign has missed no opportunity to peddle fallacious comparisons with the US system and to equate the transparency debate with a crusade against corruption.

The behaviour of the European Commission will one day make an excellent case study of how not to produce policy. From the beginning it has been all tactics and headlines, with little strategy and no sense of an ultimate destination. Commissioner Kallas has been cast in the role of a diffident Siegfried, alternatively heroic and vacuous. It is as if the old Gods of a Commission-led corporatism – the social partners, the great companies, the sprawling trade associations – sense somehow that their time is past. Strangely they have entrusted their fate not to a Wotan, but to the Sorcerer's Apprentice. This distressed pantheon includes the Member States and their national champions, frozen in immobility on their rainbow bridge. In the shadows we find scavenging Eurosceptics always keen to equate Europe with corruption and deceit.

What should we make of the performance of public affairs professionals in this evolving tragi-comedy? Clever, complex and irredeemably focused on the short term, they have been good at the public affairs of their clients and gravely inadequate in defending the legitimacy of their craft. Rich in ego, but poor in co-ordination, only in the last act are they realising their failure to communicate the purpose of public affairs. They have allowed themselves to be defined by their enemies. With rare exceptions they have failed to distinguish the different roles of consultants, trade associations and in-house practitioners. They have quibbled over codes and fussed over financial disclosure. Those who should have been seen as the life blood of democracy have come to be perceived by the public as a cross between Abramoff and Abrahams. How have we allowed the carriers of vital information between society and its political institutions to have a public profile more appropriate to a group of smokers huddled in the rain on the doorstep of democracy?

Part of the problem lies in the use and abuse of the word transparency. Transparency International is partially to blame. Its success, due in great part to skilled public relations, has permanently positioned transparency as part of the fight against corruption. Transparency is much more than that in a society in transition. Lobbyists may long for the "Tarnhelm" of invisibility, but the Facebook Generation know that there is no invisibility in the world of the 21st century. The real driver of transparency as an issue is the technology which makes privacy impossible. Those of an older generation may doubt the wisdom of sharing the details of their private lives in a public space. Facebook fans have decided to enjoy the luxury of living in the light, impervious to future employers who already prowl the new social media. No doubt in time we will all learn to live in this new world, but for the moment we are like every other generation caught in a paradigm shift – uncertain and alone.

The ETI debate has concentrated on what is described as "lobbying", despite the fact that the act of lobbying is probably about 15% of public affairs. Public affairs is a complex tapestry. The ecology of the public affairs world – the companies, the consultants, the think tanks, the churches, the

NGOs, the ministries, the civil servants, the parliamentarians – is rich and varied. Public affairs takes ideas and turns them into policies. If we could better understand how that process works, we could be honest and reject the trite model of thinking of politicians as either venal or stupid. We could recognise that politicians may not be heroes, they may be weak at times, but they are responding to a system. If we could improve that system, we would improve the quality of the outcome. Can we create a public affairs process in Europe which commands genuine public support and helps politicians do their job?

All is not lost. As in all good operas, "it ain't over till the fat lady sings". In this case the European Parliament is well cast for a dramatic appearance in the last act. The modern age of public affairs in the European Union can be accurately dated to 1979 and the first directly-elected European Parliament. Parliament's rise blew through the cosy corridors of interest representation with a cleansing zeal. Parliament shouldn't "sweat the small stuff". It matters little how much corporate entertaining is taking place on parliamentary premises. Food and drink are debased currencies in an institution rightly hungry only for information. Rather Parliament should rejoice that it is now the stage on which every issue is fought out, regardless of the details of institutional competence. Real transparency is a mixture of democracy, mandate, openness and accountability. In this game Parliament holds all the high cards.

Strangely, given the Anglo-Saxon expertise in public affairs, it is the northerners who now have key roles to play in the emerging parliamentary drama. Specific casting would be inappropriate, though Dagmar Roth-Behrendt seems chosen by the fates to play Brunhilde. How will Hans-Gert Pöttering deploy Parliament's forces? Alex Stubb and Jo Leinen played their parts well in the recent European Parliament Workshop on Lobbying. Alex brings Finnish traditions of openness and intelligent pragmatism to the minefield of a challenging Rapporteurship.

Parliament has traditionally acknowledged the usefulness of public affairs in providing the ammunition with which to amend Commission proposals and rein in the hubris of the Council. Sir Julian Priestley used to be particularly eloquent on this subject. The involvement of Parliament fundamentally changes the cramped context of the Commission proposal. Any action in this field, if it is to be effective, must embrace all three institutions. Concentrating on the Commission is pandering to its outdated vanity and is meaningless when real lobbying is at its most powerful in the interrelationship between the three institutions. A "one-stop shop" is not just a matter of convenience. Any system should also recognise that governments, both EU and external, lobby furiously and in an ideal world should be subjected to the same standards. Government representatives in the cellars of comitology and the warrens of Working Parties are central to the European public affairs process. If it is right to involve all three institutions, it must also be possible to find a legal base on which to act, or at least an Inter-Institutional Agreement.

Alex Stubb is clearly aware of this institutional geometry as Parliament's Rapporteur. We should encourage him. Proper parliamentary involvement in the debate offers the opportunity to correct some of the errors which have marred the debate so far. The Union needs separate solutions for decision-makers and for decision-influencers. Brussels could learn much from the London experience in policing the behaviour of MPs, ministers and civil servants. I have long believed that we need a Public Affairs Ombudsman to oversee public affairs practice by those seeking to influence decisions in the Union. Such a figure would take us beyond the current obsession with codes and registration. Codes of conduct are a black and white snapshot of a moving Technicolor reality. Every month something changes in the DNA of the Union. A Public Affairs Ombudsman, assisted by a panel of practitioners and stakeholders, could emulate WTO Panels in expressing best practice as it evolves. Codes are the Old Testament on tablets of stone. Our current situation demands a New Testament rooted in real transparency, if not precisely in loving one's neighbour.

Wagner's Ring starts with an embittered Albrecht renouncing love in order to acquire the Ring of Power. Such a concept rightly belongs in our shared mythic past. In the 21st century power is diffused and rests on consent. If Parliament seizes the opportunity, this music drama could yet see the Rhine swelling up to reclaim the Ring and parliamentarians, to the strains of the Ode to Liberty, laying a proper basis for a pan-European democracy.

Originally published in EU Reporter on 6 December 2007.

3. *Lobbying and the ETI: Irony and Instruction*
Steven Billet

The seemingly endless saga of the European Transparency Initiative (ETI) has been entertaining to watch over the last several years. While the debate has been predictable and mostly uninspiring, the manoeuvre of forces actually engaged in lobbying the issue has been instructive. Ironically, the actions and activities of the protagonists provide textbook illustrations of how not to lobby as well as examples of intelligent approaches to advocacy work, even from this side of the Atlantic.

Regulations inevitably create winners and losers in the political arena. Every competitive business understands that the details of regulatory regimes have different effects on different players. In many instances, it is hard to sort them out, especially when the decisions are complex compromises. Some groups see the European Transparency Initiative as a competitive threat – from the standpoint of ethereal public relations to more substantive advantages on specific policies. It explains, in some measure, the vigour of groups responding to Commissioner Kallas' effort to establish a lobbyist registration system in Europe.

The primary cleavage in the debate leading up to the voluntary regime, revealed deep differences in the two primary advocacy coalitions – reformers, pushing a system of mandatory and detailed reports for advocates; opponents, criticising the administrative burden of a regulatory regime and citing a host of competitive shortcomings in the proposal.

When the debate began, it was assumed by most that the Commission decision process would yield a regulatory regime of one kind or another and that the final decision would become the terminal act in the long drama. Indeed, a year ago the decisions facing the Commission were clear-cut and boiled down to:
- A Mandatory or Voluntary Regime;
- Full Financial Disclosure or Not;
- Defining a Lobbyist (who is covered by the regime).

The final recommendations on the ETI suggest that the anti-reform group had won on the most important issues. The regime introduced last

21

Spring would be voluntary with some incentives for signing-up. Little meaningful financial disclosure was included. Lawyers doing advocacy work would be considered lobbyists. The initial programme was rolled out in June and forms for registration and filing were posted. There were statements of warning by Commissioner Kallas made throughout the process alluding to the possible introduction of a mandatory system if the voluntary system failed.

Reaction to the voluntary regime was mixed. The Alliance for Lobbying Transparency and Ethics Regulation (ALTER-EU) was strident in its objections to the final decision. It lacked adequate financial disclosure provisions and it was a voluntary system. Their opponents were not pleased either. Some in the anti-reform community suggested that they would not participate.

Many groups registered. A review of some of the first filings showed only the barest information. Corporations, for instance, were not required to provide the names of their lobbyists, just the name of the company and a rough estimate of what their overall expenses were. No formulas were suggested to calculate financial activity, so we really had no idea if the group included total expenses to maintain their lobbying office or some percentage of the total. The reports included a listing of the issues of concern to the corporation, but there was no breakdown of what percentage of the budget went to any particular issue. As far as administrative burdens are concerned, the forms are simple and require less than an hour to complete.

The Commission issued a Code of Conduct for registrants at the same time it announced the particulars – lofty expectations, but no real teeth to assure adherence to them. Leading analysts like Tom Spencer at ECPA and Daniel Geuguen at CLAN labelled the voluntary system as useless, meaningless or a joke.

If the Kallas effort had ended there, one could have concluded that the ETI was going to fizzle out like so many earlier efforts. But the Parliament had other ideas.

The intercession of the European Parliament over the last year created a tectonic shift for the transparency issue. Late last year it became apparent the Parliament was very interested in the topic and by implication the direction of the Kallas effort. While it looked initially like they might support a voluntary approach, they gravitated to a posture more reflective of the positions of ALTER-EU. Their final report contained definitive departures from the Commission voluntary regime.

The Parliament's position focused on the legitimacy of the EU's institutions, noting that the public should find it easy to secure information about what influences interest representatives are having on decisions. Their report recommends important changes to the transparency regime:
- That the Parliament, the Commission and the Council adopt a "one-stop shop" registration system where one registration mechanism will serve all three bodies;
- That the EU adopt a mandatory registry;
- That the financial disclosure requirements for registrants be clarified;
- That each action taken by an institution includes a "legislative footprint", basically a list of interest groups that consulted with the institution during consideration of a measure.

The obstacles between the present situation and an agreement among the Commission, Council and Parliament are formidable. The intervention of the Parliament into the decision arena has muddied the waters on the issue. It has introduced the possibility of a much more rigorous, mandatory regime for the whole of the EU. The debate has been opened on a new front and will likely extend for some years to come. In the meantime, the voluntary Commission version of transparency is in its "beta" phase.

A confounding variable facing all the groups interested in the topic is the changing faces of players on the pitch. Commissioner Kallas will be gone before a final evaluation of the voluntary system is rendered. While many have complained about his approach and the outcomes, he should be praised for his persistence in shepherding a tough issue through an elongated process. It would have been easy to throw his hands up in the air and walk away from it. Who knows who will get the portfolio in the next Commission or if the next Commission and its President will support it?

At the same time, Alexander Stubb has left the Parliament and moved on to the foreign ministry in Finland. As the prime mover of the Parliament's efforts on transparency, he moved the debate toward a more inclusive, detailed and compulsory direction. While there are others in the

Parliament seemingly committed to the EP's position, it is still unclear if they will be able to drive the process to conclusion.

Against this backdrop, we have witnessed lobbyists lobbying about the content of a lobbying regime. It is often said that there are two things you never want to watch being made: sausage and law. In this case, I would have preferred the sausage. It has not been a pretty thing, especially when one considers the particulars of the lobbying campaigns.

Lesson One: Evident Strategies . . . and Not

The interim outcome described above suggests that there was little consideration given to the question of advocacy strategy by the anti-reform group. Their reaction was, in large part, to simply react and oppose, raising a variety of objections to the whole notion of a transparency regime. Given the history of previous failed initiatives, it is not surprising that they anticipated a similar outcome this time around. Given the hurdles a regime still faces between now and final implementation, some might suggest that this approach continues to have some merit. I disagree.

Having a goal of just "killing off" a proposal like the ETI is not much of a strategy, particularly given the consensus-seeking policy environment in the EU. It was clear that the approach of the anti-reformers did not: 1) identify a clearly stated goal, 2) develop and co-ordinate a broad approach to the process, 3) develop and communicate a "fall-back" position (until the process had passed them by).

Lesson Two: Expand the Arena

From the outset, it was clear that Commissioner Kallas preferred a voluntary, minimalist registration system for EU lobbyists. While there were occasional threats about making the system mandatory, the Commission never seriously embraced the position. The final decision was generally consistent with the wishes of many that had profound reservations with the ETI and fell well short of the position of ALTER-EU and other reformers.

If the process had played out as envisioned, the Commission would have put its regime in place and lobbyists of all kinds would have registered (or not). We would have revisited the issue at some point after assessments were rendered on the effectiveness of the programme.

The reform community led by ALTER-EU understood and took advantage of one of the most basic tactical imperatives in lobbying: "When you are about to lose on an issue, expand the arena". Induce other, friendly institutions, interests or parties to get involved. The European Parliament certainly changed the calculus of the transparency initiative. Their work in early 2008 moved the issue, side-stepping the Commission's work. While the European Parliament was almost certain to interject itself into the ETI, they got lots of encouragement from the reformers. It is clear too, that Alexander Stubb's position on transparency evolved over the last year from one of general acceptance of a voluntary register to one supporting mandatory registration.

This phenomenon is nothing new to practitioners and academics alike. E.E. Schattschneider recognised it in his work, *The Semisovereign People*. He noted that in situations of political conflict, there are two parties, the protagonists and the interested audience. Nothing, according to Schattschneider, is so contagious or compelling as a fight and the best thing a loser can do is bring the audience into the conflict on their side.

Lesson Three: Concede on Principle

The ETI's naysayers had manifold issues with the whole idea of a transparency regime. Many were not just opposed to a mandatory system, they did not want any system of lobbyist registration. They groused and griped about burdensome forms. They complained about revealing sensitive competitor data. They asked for "carve-outs" for their "special circumstances".

Some of the least enlightened of the whining came from the Society of European Affairs Professionals (SEAP). As the Commission began to solidify the ETI, SEAP issued a threat that it might advise its members to boycott the ETI; that it saw so little merit in the whole programme that they would tell their members to defy the Commission and not participate. Of all the positions taken by groups through the many months leading up to the programme, this was the most perplexing and played straight into the hands of the reform community.

What should SEAP have done? Easy, "concede on the principle and fight it out when it came to the details of the programme". Anyone who has been awake for the last few years understood that Kallas' little project had legs and that this issue was not going to just go away. If they were paying any attention to the Brussels political scene beyond their own boardrooms, and engaged in something other than a self-serving assessment, they would have seen that the reform community had become increasingly vocal and progressively effective.

Eventually, SEAP and two other important players, the European Centre for Public Affairs (ECPA) and the European Public Affairs Consultancies' Association (EPACA) came together and signed a joint statement addressed to the President of the European Parliament, the President of the European Commission and the President in Office of the Council. The letter indicated support for the development of a single register for interest representatives for all three institutions of the EU. It acknowledges in closing (conceding on principle) that the three organisations are committed to working "to create an open and credible working environment for public affairs in the EU". But by threatening to opt out of the ETI, SEAP put itself and its members on the margins of the debate.

Lesson Four: Unrelenting Pressure

Over the years, the public affairs and political environment in Brussels has changed decisively. Just a decade ago, it was a relic of the neo-corporatist interest group model. Conflict was minimised or muted and the positions of interests on any given issue were compromised in a consensus-seeking milieu. It was comfortable, even cozy; an insiders' game.

The entry and growth of the NGO community has had an enormous impact on the way policies get made in Brussels. They undermine the now-tattered neo-corporatist ethic of the EU, bringing more confrontation, fundamental to pluralist interest group activity.

ALTER-EU's activities on the ETI are instructive for anyone interested in lobbying strategy and tactics.

First, ALTER-EU was a big coalition with over 150 organisations represented in the group. Its members included some of the behemoths of the NGO arena as well as many smaller groups. Building, maintaining and coordinating activity for a broad coalition like ALTER-EU is a demanding job. They have done it well thus far on this issue.

Second, ALTER-EU had a message and stuck with it since the ETI first emerged. If you examine the first statements of the group and some of the most recent statements they are nearly identical. ALTER-EU had a disciplined, consistent message – a lesson for anyone engaged in political advocacy.

Third, ALTER-EU was absolutely relentless and uncompromising in its approach to the issue. There was never an inkling that they might cave in, compromise or equivocate.

This last point should be a most important lesson for advocates and instructive for people interested in learning more about the lobbying style of the NGO community. Many of the groups in ALTER-EU have roots in leftist advocacy of the US. Many of these groups, thoroughly pluralist and confrontational, were spawned and animated by activist Saul Alinsky, author of a book entitled *Rules for Radicals*. Alinsky is considered the Godfather of grassroots for the American left. While most of the NGO operatives in Europe probably have no idea who Alinsky was, they know well two of his tactical rules. The first is to "keep the pressure on" – unrelenting, unyielding, insistent. Never accept a compromise since the opposition is the incarnation of the devil; 100% evil. Second, the approach is aggressive, suggesting that operatives "Pick the target, freeze it, personalise it, and polarise it". This is the polar opposite of consensus building and one of the reasons the anti-reform community is so disturbed by the rise of the NGO community. Consider the purpose and function of the asinine "Worst Lobbyist Award".

Lesson Five: Sometimes a Great Notion...

When advocates are honest with themselves, they can distinguish between real and contrived issues and political movements. It comes instinctively. They recognise that even in situations where an issue comes up repeatedly, there will be one time where the stars align just so. They develop a visceral feel for things political and through intelligent calculation know an "idea whose time has come". It's easy for lobbyists to overlook these signals when they appear. We get so accustomed to manipulating opinion, stage-managing campaigns and controlling political situations, we think we can do it on every issue. Lobbyists get paid to do just that and many do it well.

With the ETI it would be easy to suppose that this effort would result in the same insincere and hollow promises associated with earlier efforts to build a registration scheme for the EU. We have seen them come and go. They have had no appreciable impact, producing, in the end, cynical public reaction, diminished standing for the EU's institutions and opprobrium for the lobbying community.

But every so often an issue comes up and we just know that this is the moment when it is going to pass. While ALTER-EU may have been driven more by belief than fact, they did in the end, position themselves more effectively to advance the ETI in a direction they favoured. Others, probably expecting yet another failed effort at lobbying regulation, did not give enough attention to the issue to have a serious impact.

4. *The Context and Inspiration of the European Transparency Initiative*

Kristian Schmidt

Let me start with some general remarks about how the European Commission sees lobbying. First of all, the Commission believes society should recognise lobbying as legitimate and necessary. In a democracy, active private involvement in setting public priorities is an asset. In return, we believe society can expect lobbying to be transparent. So for me, "lobbying" is not a dirty word. I use the term in a very broad sense, covering any activity intended to influence the decision-making process of public authorities. This means that the Commission defines public affairs professionals, law firms, trade unions, NGOs, think tanks, companies and professional associations as lobbyists, or "interest representatives", a term that in some countries has less negative associations in the public. For these entities, the European Commission runs a voluntary register since June 2008, with currently 437 entities registered.

It is important to set out the context and inspiration we used in developing this model. The first observation is that not much has been done to regulate lobbying in the EU Member States. None of the 15 "old" EU Member States have regulated lobbying, although some are discussing it. For instance, the UK House of Commons is conducting an inquiry into the matter, considering whether to abandon the current system entirely relying on self-regulation. My own country, Denmark, while advocating a mandatory register at EU level, has nothing at the national level.

Looking at some of the 12 new EU Member States that joined the EU in 2004 and 2007, the situation is as follows[1]:
- In Bulgaria, Slovenia, Estonia, Romania, Slovakia, and Latvia, lobbying is entirely unregulated. In Romania and Slovakia, ambitious regulatory proposals were in fact tabled in the past, but were then rejected in parliamentary votes.
- Only three EU Member States – Hungary, Poland and Lithuania – have in fact passed statutory regulation, but I know there are doubts about their effectiveness. Lithuania passed US style legislation in 2000,

---

1. This section draws on McGrath, C. (2008) "The Development and Regulation of Lobbying in the New Member States of the European Union", *Journal of Public Affairs*, 8(1/2), pp. 15-32.

with a system of "accreditation" for a license to lobby. Apparently, only seven entities are registered, and enforcement is said to be limited. Poland also requires professional lobbyists to register, but only 11 have done so, and it seems unofficial lobbying continues undeterred.

Still, it seems new Member States are more concerned, and more likely to legislate. This is not surprising, and was fully confirmed in a study done for the European Commission on regulation of conflicts of interest. This study clearly showed that the new Member States were more likely to resort to regulatory solutions, whereas the old Member States relied on common sense and ethics[2]. Apparently, in countries emerging from communism, legislators are rightly keen to eradicate all forms of secrecy, corruption and conflicts of interest. This desire for openness and transparency certainly drives my own commissioner, Vice-president Siim Kallas. He is from Estonia, a country that reacquired its independence from the Soviet Union not too long ago...

So let me make one perhaps surprising remark at this point – one that may go against public perception. During economic and political transition, open lobbying is probably a healthy sign of positive democratic change. Communism discouraged independent civic activity, and in economic life, with large state-owned monopolies rejecting reform or privatization, small and medium-sized enterprises may have to unite in businesses association to be heard. A survey of transition countries actually found that lobbying and corruption are reversely related, in the sense that the more corrupt a nation is, the less likely individual firms are to engage in lobbying[3].

So the alternative to open, professional lobbying is not no lobbying. The alternative is informal or secret lobbying, through "fixers" and "contacts" through someone who knows the right public officials and is willing to try to influence them, for instance on public procurement contracts. This is a recipe for corruption. It is better to recognize that interests will be pursued in any case, and to do so in an open manner.

To be completely transparent, I should reveal that the European Commission – in developing our model – was inspired by the American

---

2. Demmke, C. et al. (2007) "Regulating Conflicts of Interest for Holders of Public Office in the European Union: A Comparative Study of the Rules and Standards of Professional Ethics for the Holders of Public Office in the EU-27 and EU Institutions", Maastricht: European Institute of Public Administration.
3. Campos, N.F. and Giovannoni, F. (2007) "Lobbying, Corruption and Political Influence", *Public Choice*, 131(1/2), pp. 1-21.

experience. To explain what we learned from that, let me briefly go back 70 years – to the US in 1938, when lobbying regulation started. In 1938, President Roosevelt believed Hitler was supporting a US Nazi movement to make the US stay out of the pending war in Europe. In response, Roosevelt developed the Foreign Agents Registration Act (FARA) as a lobbying disclosure law[4].

In 1946, Congress extended disclosure to domestic lobbyists through the Federal Regulation of Lobbying Act. This law required anyone whose "principal purpose" was lobbying, to register and file quarterly financial reports, identifying paying clients and amounts; publications printed; and legislation he was attempting to influence. Although detailed and strict, these laws were judged as a failure. Many simply chose to consider their "principal purpose" as something other than lobbying. In 1991, out of an estimated 13,500 entries in the *Directory of Washington Representatives*, 10,000 were not registered[5].

So in 1995, the US Congress went further, enacting the Lobbying Disclosure Act. Discretion was reduced, and "principal purpose" was defined as more than 20% of your time spent on "lobbying activities" over a three-month period[6]. But this was also considered a failure, because it did not set up a system of electronic filing and disclosure to the public. You could not search the files, and NGOs and journalists found it of limited use to uncover corruption.

In 2005, the Jack Abramoff scandals eventually rocked Capitol Hill, and in the 2006 elections, the National Election Pool's exit polls indicated that "corruption and scandal in government" was the single most important issue to the voters – considered more important than terrorism. In 2007, Congress responded with the Honest Leadership and Open Government Act – the most sweeping lobbying and ethics reforms in decades. This new Act finally established a fully searchable and downloadable electronic disclosure database on the Internet. It also covers gifts and free travel, prohibiting the infamous

> 4. The FARA register still exists today. The records have since been made public on a website hosted by the US Department of Justice at <http://www.usdoj.gov/criminal/fara/>.
> 5. General Accounting Office (1991) "Federal Lobbying: Federal Regulation of Lobbying Act of 1946 is Ineffective". In the study, GAO interviewed a sample of those identified in Washington Representatives and found that 75% had contacted both members of Congress and their staffs, dealt with federal legislation, and sought to influence Congress or the Executive Branch.
> 6. "Lobbying activities" were defined as "contacts and efforts in support of such contacts, including preparation and planning activities, research and other background work that is intended, at the time it is performed, for use in contacts, and coordination with the lobbying activities of others."

golf trips to Scotland and the Super Bowl tickets which former lobbyist Jack Abramoff used to impress and influence lawmakers.

The rules are very detailed. To give just two examples, they specify that "finger food" is allowed at "widely attended" events; or lobbyists may pay for one-day trips for lawmakers attending a conference or making a speech, provided these trips are pre-approved by a congressional ethics committee, and provided the sponsors, cost and itineraries are posted on the Internet. Not surprisingly, many American lobbyists consider these new rules intrusive. So are they are a model for Europe?

First of all, Mr Kallas believes we can learn a lot from the US experience. The main lesson is this: if you wish to force lobbyists to change their ways against their own free will, you need some pretty intrusive rules. In the US, 70 years of increasingly detailed regulation did not prevent a scandal, which undermined public trust, changed the political landscape and made contacts with lobbyists a controversial element in the current Presidential elections.

For these reasons, among others, the Commission did not just copy the US approach. Acting preventively, before a scandal, we chose to give the profession the benefit of the doubt – an opportunity to preserve the current open relations without imposing bureaucratic barriers and heavy reporting requirements. We made it voluntary first. Mr Kallas certainly did not refrain from proposing mandatory registration because he thought it would not fly politically. Events have shown during the course of the debate that it would fly perfectly well. There would be an instant majority in the European Parliament in favour of mandatory registration. His reasons are more principled. He sees the European Transparency Initiative as an opportunity for *bona fide* lobbyists to step into the light.

Lobbying is part of a freedom of expression, and Mr Kallas does not want to criminalise it. On the contrary, we formally recognised lobbying as "necessary and legitimate". So the European approach is to try to put a bonus on transparency. In the US approach, the legislation puts a penalty on getting caught. This puts a huge burden on the legislator, and to be credible, you need enforcement procedures and significant resources. This seems difficult so far in some of the new EU Member States following this model.

The Commission has decided to follow a middle path. We have not started with heavy legislation, but nor will we sit and wait for a catastrophe to happen, and then legislate in a hurry. The purpose of the European Transparency Initiative is to preserve and enhance public trust in EU institutions by preventing such scandals from happening, in co-operation with the lobbyists themselves. Critics have called this naïve, and some NGOs call our register "a smokescreen" for mandatory transparency. Craig Holman of Public Citizen, an American watchdog group, recently said that "a real system of transparency means that someone who wants to hide in the shadows cannot. If disclosure is optional, transparency is lost".

But is this true? Can any piece of legislation eliminate the shadows? Some experts on lobbying in Washington claim the latest US lobbying reform has simply changed the location of that shadow. As one Washington-based lobbyist puts it; "We will adapt to the changing environment, as we have adapted before". Jack Abramoff himself said he "lived in the loopholes" [of the law]. To think we can cover all loopholes is probably to underestimate the creativity of the lobbying profession! And that would be naïve!

These are the reasons behind our approach. The onus is on lobbyists to manage the reputation of their profession. Mr Kallas launched this debate in November 2005 and the Commission consulted widely. We got the feedback that the profession was, in fact, willing to collaborate. So we formulated a proposal and after public consultations, the Commission opened a voluntary register in June 2008.

Contrary to the US, we're not asking for individual lobbyists to be named. This may come later, if we agree with the European Parliament on a "one-stop shop". We do, however, ask for financial disclosure. Interest representatives are asked to disclose their estimated expenditures on lobbying activity per year in broad ranges of €50,000. Public affairs companies have to reveal the identity of their clients, and their relative weight in the overall turnover of the consultancy. Registration also requires compliance with an ethics code, either the one recommended by the Commission, or an internal one, provided it has equivalent requirements.

In summary, our model is voluntary, because there is no legislative or statutory text. But it goes well beyond self-regulation, because it is the

Commission that runs the registers; has committed to effective enforcement and sanctions, where justified; has adopted the obligatory code of conduct and set the obligatory minimum information required to join the register; and – finally – clearly announced mandatory registration if our gentle persuasion to join us voluntarily is not heard. So far, 437 entities have already registered, saying they found it easy to do. Many others are preparing to register, and my overall impression is that the voluntary approach is working.

Originally delivered as a speech to a conference on 'The Importance of Regulating Lobbying in Croatia', convened by the Croatian Society of Lobbyists in October 2008.

5. *The Continuing ETI Process: The Genesis, Functioning and Future of the Commission's Register for Interest Representatives*

Jens Nymand Christensen

Right after the assumption of office, the Commissioners under the leadership of President José Manuel Barroso agreed on the importance of maintaining the Commission as an open, accessible and accountable institution. Echoing the pledge in Article 1 of the Treaty on European Union to take decisions "as openly as possible and as closely as possible to the citizens", the Commission therefore stressed, in its Strategic Objectives 2005-2009 (COM(2005)12 final), the importance of a "high level of transparency" to ensure that the Union is "open to public scrutiny and accountable for its work". As a follow-up to this commitment, Vice President Kallas launched a debate about the so-called European Transparency Initiative (ETI), leading first to a Green Paper and, later on, to two Communications. With this Initiative, the European Commission led the way, establishing, among other measures, a new framework for the relations that interest representatives (lobbyists) maintain with the European institutions. While ETI is a much more comprehensive programme, it is on the framework for interest representation that this essay focuses.

Brussels as a Black Box? The Need for a European Transparency Initiative

The Initiative and the Commission's motivation behind it were not always fully understood. The Commission acted on its own initiative and not because a big lobbying scandal had occurred, pushing public authorities to adopt tough measures to calm public opinion. Indeed, relations between lobbyists and the Commission had always been based on mutual respect and confidence: interest representatives knew that the Commission, being an open and accessible institution, would consider their contributions seriously. On the other hand, the Commission knew that lobbyists represent their interests decently – its officials therefore didn't have any reason to distrust their inputs. It was – and still is – a virtuous circle.

However, the system was only working well insofar as there were no scandals. The situation was less positive when it came to its perception by (in particular) European citizens. Some in Brussels and even more in the Member States had the feeling that European lobbying is a black box. Citizens outside the microcosm didn't know what was going on. And they had no possibility of finding out who was acting and with what aims. On the ground of such ignorance, myths, suspicion and mistrust could grow. Even if unfairly, at best, Brussels was seen as an inaccessible political place, where all sorts of measures were taken obscurely. At worst, the Commission was considered as detached Eurocrats, creating legislation only for the good of special interests. Limiting the reaction to those critics to a simple statement that "Everything is fine, don't worry!" was not enough – a better and more convincing answer was needed.

This situation was far too paradoxical to be allowed to continue. Everybody involved in the decision-making process encountered distrust, although there was nothing to hide. All – be they public affairs practitioners, officials or politicians – were regarded with suspicion, and yet there had been no lobbying scandal. As the Commissioners believed that openness and honesty are the best ways of combating prejudice, they decided to open that "black box" in order to prove that there was nothing to hide: the European Transparency Initiative was born. It is designed to combat the myths, the ignorance and the suspicion and regain people's trust by improving the transparency of the European Union's decision-making processes.

Another *raison d'être* of the European Transparency Initiative was the steady evolution of the Commission towards a more open and accessible institution. The involvement of stakeholders has been greatly reinforced over the years – the Commission has become more transparent and permeable. The other side of the coin is that the Commission expects stakeholders to improve their transparency, too: with better involvement comes greater responsibility.

A Useful, Important and Legitimate Activity: The Commission's Perception of Lobbying

To underline that ETI was not established as a sign of mistrust against the lobbyists, but created also as an opportunity for them to improve the reputation of their profession, the Commission stated repeatedly the usefulness, the importance and the legitimacy of interest representation.

Indeed, one can consider that there is a triple imperative for decision-makers to listen to lobbyists.

First and foremost, it is <u>a democratic imperative</u>. The Commission considers it normal in a democracy that you try to influence decisions when you are concerned by what is at stake. We live in societies where citizens are free to say what they think about the policies being shaped by their democratic institutions. And, of course, lobbyists are free to do so, too. As with all democratic institutions, the European Commission relies on ongoing popular support. It is only by listening to its constituency that it can be responsive: this ensures that European policies live up to the expectations of the Europeans. Listening to citizens is rewarded, in turn, by public support. Therefore and in order to get a balanced picture, the Commission listens to all those who want to express their opinion. Then, the democratically legitimated Commissioners decide on how to go ahead, with the sole aim of serving the general interest of the European Union and its citizens.

Second, it is <u>a practical imperative</u>, to listen to lobbyists, representing the addressees of legislation before it is actually shaped. This is particularly true when you bear in mind the Commission's Better Regulation Agenda. The Commission needs to submit proposals to the legislative bodies that respond to the needs of those who will be concerned by that legislation. That is why it is imperative to listen to those who are the experts in their fields. Their points of view can complete and enrich the expertise of the Commission's services. And this is precisely why lobbyists can help in improving the quality of legislative proposals.

One could add that listening to lobbyists is <u>a legal imperative</u>, too. There is actually a legal obligation to listen to stakeholders before drafting legislative proposals. A protocol of the Treaty of Amsterdam states that "the Commission should consult widely before proposing legislation and, wherever appropriate, publish consultation documents".

Based on the triple conviction that there was a need to act, that lobbying is a legitimate activity and that both the public administration and interest representatives had an interest in improving the transparency of the whole procedure, the Commission established a unique framework which combines regulatory measures with elements of self-regulation.

The Register: A Unique Combination of Regulation and Self-Regulation

Registration is indeed voluntary, but organisations signing up have to adhere to a Code of Conduct whose purpose is to regulate the relations between lobbyists and the European Commission and they agree to give certain information. The information the Commission asks for provides a clearer picture of who acts, with what motivation, objectives and missions and against what financial background.

When it comes to the financial disclosure, one can observe the combination of regulatory and self-regulatory elements. Indeed, the Commission has clearly defined which figures must be published, leaving it, however, to the registrants to establish a methodology on how to assess the figures.

This decision was guided by the philosophy of the Commission's Better Regulation agenda: desiring to avoid any unnecessary administrative burden and considering that the lobbyists themselves would certainly know their business best, the Commission trusted that either the interest representatives individually or their European networks would find a coherent and pertinent way to evaluate their financial effort to influence the European institutions. The developments so far seem to confirm that the Commission was right. Rather than elaborating very detailed rules for each category as seen in some other systems, it has left it to the lobbyists within the given parameters to develop a method of registration that corresponds best to their particular situation. It has taken a bit of time but nothing seen so far indicates that it has proven excessively burdensome for potential registrants. The Commission has remained available throughout the period with guidance and answers to any specific questions.

Critics said that this combined approach of regulatory and self-regulatory elements would not work and that the Commission was naïve in creating a semi-voluntary system and in counting on the abilities of the lobbyists.

The facts of the past months proved the critics wrong: first of all, registrations are coming in steadily and from all categories. Even organisations that were very critical at the beginning have changed their minds and have signed up or prepare to do so. They have understood that they cannot afford to be considered as not supporting the Commission's efforts on transparency. Not only the public, but also Commission staff might increasingly feel that lobbyists outside the Register could have something to hide, preferring to remain in the dark. This is something any honourable lobbyist would surely seek to avoid: his or her reputation would suffer. Clients will also increasingly ask themselves the question who will most efficiently represent their interests in Brussels, somebody within or somebody outside the Register?

For the same reasons, no interest representative would dare to give wrong figures or consciously underestimate a given lobbying effort: being caught doing so would also cause long-lasting damage to their reputation.

The result of all this is that the current discussions are no longer turning around the question of whether there is a need for a Register or whether there should be financial disclosure. The principle of a Register to improve transparency is widely acknowledged and this important cultural change has been accepted by all relevant players. Today, the questions are focussing on "how best to sign up" – this important step ahead confirms the Commission's approach and is deeply encouraging.

From Detectives, North-Sea Women and the European Consumers

The first months of existence of the Register have already given an unprecedented level of transparency. Citizens can now see the huge diversity and multitude of organisations, companies, public affairs consultants, NGOs and think-tanks active in representing their interests in Brussels. This underlines impressively that it is not only "Big Business" and powerful NGOs that influence decisions in Brussels – the picture is much more diverse and complex. Who would have thought that the "Bundesverband Deutscher Detektive e.V.", the German Federal Association of Detectives, has been representing its interests *vis-à-vis* the European Commission? Who would have imagined that the "North Sea Women's Network" has become active to speak within Europe for women and families living in coastal communities? Still, those organisations are registered, along with better known actors in Brussels such as Burson-Marsteller or BEUC, the European Consumers' Organisation.

Despite this reassuring finding, the glass remains half empty. Whereas some categories are well represented, others have still quite a way to go. Law firms, companies, public affairs consultancies and think-tanks are still especially under-represented. In that respect, the six-step checklist ECPA has published is an important step in the right direction – as it is intended to facilitate registration.

As several organisations have prepared comparable guidelines and as others are finalising their documents, the Commission expects a large number of new registrations before the Christmas break. It is still too early to give an answer to the question of whether the Register is a success or not. In Spring 2009, the Commission will assess how the framework is working and adjust it where necessary. Obviously, one of the elements will be the participation rate, in the Register, of interest representatives active in Brussels. If this rate proves to be too low, the Commission has always said that it would consider taking new measures to ensure that more interest representatives would sign up.

Registration as a Win-Win-Win Situation

For the time being however, the Commission remains cautiously confident, expecting the figures to keep growing. Indeed, registration is a win-win-win situation: it benefits the public, because they will gain greater insight into, and better understanding of, these processes. It benefits the European Commission, as it has been proven that transparent institutions produce better results. And it benefits the interest representatives, as they are publicly declaring that they are prepared to accept the new rules of the game and that they have nothing to hide.

6. *A Framework for Lobbyists in the European Institutions*

Ingo Friedrich MEP

Lobbying as Part of the Decision-Making Process

Despite its often negative connotation, lobbying is an important element in the decision-making process of democratic systems. By allowing any kind of public or private interest representatives to express their views and to contribute to the legislative process, lobbyism offers the opportunity for an open and pluralistic dialogue.

Lobbying means primarily providing information, it is not about negative influencing or corruption. Lobbyists give decision-makers highly valuable expert knowledge. In their legislative work, Members of the European Parliament are often dealing with very detailed and technical questions, about environmental standards for example. Of course decision-makers have to listen to different interest representatives to get a balanced view on an issue. But getting information from different lobbyists, and seeing the issue from different perspectives, enables MEPs to make qualified choices. Therefore sincere and transparent lobbyism enhances the effectiveness of decision-making.

Transparent Regulations for the EU Parliament

Lobbyists attempt to influence Parliament's decision-making processes by lobbying its Members and their assistants, political group staff and also officials working in the secretariats of the parliamentary committees. However to guarantee the benefits of lobbyism, clear and transparent rules are needed to regulate the behaviour and the admission of lobbyists to the Parliament and its employees. To prevent unfair methods, all kind of interest groups must have equal access to decision-makers.

In 1996 the European Parliament introduced a register for lobbyists in its premises. All registered lobbyists have to sign the Code of Conduct, which includes a commitment to act in accordance with high ethical standards. They have to disclose for which organisation they work, and are forbidden to obtain information by fraud or to sell copies of documents they got in the Parliament. Currently, 5,000 registered lobbyists have regular access to the building, committee meetings, conferences and hearings.

Responding to the "European Transparency Initiative" launched by the Commission, the European Parliament has furthermore adopted a resolution on the "Development of the Framework for the Activities of Interest Representatives (Lobbyists) in the European Institutions". This own-initiative report was approved in plenary on 8 May 2008. By doing this, the Parliament has adopted a broad definition of lobbyists including all public and private interest representatives outside the EU institutions such as professional lobbyists, companies' in-house lobbyists, NGOs, think-tanks etc. Within this group, there are no first or second class lobbyists. All interest representatives have the same rights and duties. However, regions and municipalities of Member States, parties and churches are not considered as lobbyists as they are granted a specific status by the Treaties.

The new framework aims at improving the Parliament's transparency regarding lobbyists and proposes the introduction of a so-called "legislative footprint". In order to disclosure which knowledge and interests have been incorporated, the Rapporteur may, on a voluntary basis, attach to official reports an indicative list of registered interest representatives who were consulted, and had significant input during the preparation of the document. Eventually, lobbyists will not perceive this list as an undesirable disclosure, but being on the list will mean having lobbied successfully.

Common Rules for the European Parliament and Commission

In its resolution, the Parliament also wants to define a general framework for lobbyist activities in the European institutions. To promote transparency but also to keep bureaucratic burdens on lobbyists at a reasonable level, the Parliament's proposal supports a "one-stop shop", a common lobbyists' register for the Council, Commission and Parliament. The common register will contain separate categories in which lobbyists will be registered according to the type of interests they represent (e.g. professional associations, company representatives, trade unions, employers' organisations, law firms, NGOs). The register should be mandatory and will include a common code of ethical behaviour. The major improvement compared to the current Parliament register will be the new request of financial transparency. Lobbyists will have to provide full financial disclosure when registering. For a professional consultancy, this could mean revealing the turnover of its lobbying activities and the relative weight of its main clients. Companies or trade associations will have to estimate the costs associated with direct lobbying of the EU institutions. NGOs and think-tanks must disclose their overall budget and the main sources of funding. These figures can be verified by the institutions. As it will be a public register, also the press or competitors can contest the figures put forward by a lobbying group. Wrong figures or breaches of the Code of Conduct will entail sanctions such as suspension from the register, and in more serious cases removal from the register.

The Parliament proposed to set up a working group, consisting of high-ranking members of the Parliament, Council and Commission which is supposed to discuss the details of a common register. The working group should start its work in autumn 2008 with representatives of the Parliament and the Commission. Being less concerned by lobbying activities, the Council decided at the moment not to participate at the negotiations for a common register. The target is to launch the register after the European elections in 2009.

It is however important that the Commission adopted a more transparent approach regarding lobbyists dealing with its officials. As this institution has a powerful position, being at the same time the initiator and executive of European legislation, its employees are highly demanded interlocutors of lobbyists. Therefore in its resolution, the European Parliament recommended to the Commission to introduce as well a "legislative footprint" to explain which lobbyists contributed to its legislative proposals. In summer 2008, the Commission launched a first register including financial disclosure for lobbyists being in contact with Commission officials. It is a public web-based register, easily accessible for everyone via the Internet. So far the Commission register is voluntary, but the future common register could be based on this model. The aim is to develop an efficient but also user-friendly register to professionalise relations with lobbyists in the European institutions. Being on the list should be a sign of quality for lobbyists proving that they are serious and trustworthy partners.

The Relationship with Lobbyists: A Difficult Balance

Lobbyists are interested in good and stable relations with decision-makers. They want to gain a permanent interlocutor who takes the time to listen to their arguments. The better the relationship is, the more chances lobbyists have to get a personal meeting with decision-makers. Aggressive lobbying is not appreciated and often counterproductive. Unsound behaviour and corruption is forbidden by the Code of Conduct. Of course these rules can not prevent criminal energies but to reveal these, we need hints from colleagues or the press.

It is the personal responsibility of every decision-maker not to accept any dubious offer, but I can tell from my own experience that I never had one. As a Member of the European Parliament, you are not allowed to accept any gift of value. In practice, we get small give-aways, pens, wine bottles or books which are often passed to assistants or *stagiaires*. Also invitations to expensive restaurants are not useful to attract the attention and votes of MEPs. Once a German association invited all 99 German parliamentarians to one of the most expensive restaurants in Brussels, but only three MEPs attended the event. I was one of them and I had to leave after the first course due to a later appointment. European parliamentarians have a tight schedule; so generally, I meet lobbyists for breakfast or lunch in the Members' restaurant in the Parliament or in my office. In the end, you get a paper with a summary of their position. These are serene and factual conversations for mutual information. It is not a marketplace where the partners negotiate deals and return services. But it is difficult to maintain the balance between good relations with lobbyists and the independence to keep as an elected representative.

The project of a common register for the European Parliament and Commission has to be seen as a first step for transparent lobbying in the EU institutions. We will use the experience gained through the current Parliament register and the recently introduced Commission register. Of course there will still be gaps and points that could be improved. Therefore the register and the general framework for lobbyist activities should be regularly evaluated in order to close gaps bit by bit.

7. *Transparency and the European Ombudsman*
P. Nikiforos Diamandouros

The European Ombudsman deals with complaints against the EU institutions and bodies. As Ombudsman, my main focus is on ensuring that the EU administration respects the law, adheres to the principles of good administration, and ensures respect for fundamental rights. An open, high quality and well-functioning EU administration is of particular importance to European affairs practitioners, since it enhances their capacity to carry out their work effectively.

European Transparency Initiative

The biggest single issue that gives rise to Ombudsman inquiries is lack of transparency. Almost one-third of all our inquiries concern failure to provide adequate information. This underlines the importance of projects such as the Commission's European Transparency Initiative. The stated aim of this Initiative is to make the European Union and its institutions more open and accountable.

Transparency and democratic accountability go hand in hand. The basic idea of transparency is that citizens should easily be able to obtain the information they need in order to call public authorities to account. Transparency implies that public authorities should be proactive in publishing information, in ways that can be easily understood by the intended audience. In addition, transparency requires public authorities to react promptly and, as far as possible, positively to requests from members of the public for access to information and documents which have not yet been published.

One of the concerns driving the European Transparency Initiative is the need to combat corruption. I am convinced, and all experience shows, that greater transparency and openness in the public administration is negatively correlated with levels of corruption. An open and transparent public administration makes it more difficult to hide corrupt practices. My contribution as European Ombudsman to combating corruption lies mainly in my work promoting greater openness and transparency in the EU administration, and seeking to attain greater accountability among the EU institutions and bodies.

Since the European Transparency Initiative was launched, I have followed its development closely. I have made clear that I believe that one of the most effective ways to increase trust in the Union and its administration is to improve transparency. I was greatly encouraged, for example, by moves to make data on beneficiaries of EU funds more transparent. The idea that Member States should disclose information on who receives EU money is certainly a step in the right direction. As Ombudsman, I have received complaints about lack of transparency in the field of beneficiaries of EU funds. My view is that it is in the general public interest to provide information on how EU taxpayers' money is spent. Explaining openly what the EU and the Member States do in the name of the citizen makes the European Union more democratic and accessible.

It is for this reason that I welcomed the decision of the European Parliament to publish general information on MEPs' allowances on its website. While I believe that Parliament should have gone further, its acknowledgment that the public has the right to know how MEPs spend public money is an important step forward.

Serving as the Guardian of Transparency

Since the establishment of the institution, the European Ombudsman has striven for a more open and democratic European Union. Many of the European Ombudsman's achievements in promoting transparency are linked to inquiries into allegations of refusal of access to documents and information. Complaints that my office has dealt with in this area have helped to make a real difference.

In terms of contesting decisions taken under the EU's public access to documents rules (namely, Regulation 1049/2001[1]), the Regulation gives applicants a choice of remedy: they may challenge a refusal of access either in court proceedings, or by way of complaint to the Ombudsman. In making their choice, citizens will no doubt take into account that there is no cost in going to the Ombudsman, no need to have a lawyer, and we are normally quicker in dealing with cases than a Court. On the other hand, I have no power to annul a decision refusing access.

---

1. Regulation (EC) No. 1049/2001 of the European Parliament and of the Council of 30 May 2001 regarding public access to European Parliament, Council and Commission documents: OJ 2001 L 145, p. 43.

Let me give an example of a case that illustrates the application of these rules and the Ombudsman's efforts to promote further transparency. I criticised the Commission for its refusal to grant access to documents it had submitted to the WTO on scientific concerns about the safety of genetically modified foods. This followed a complaint by the environmental NGO, Friends of the Earth, which had asked the Commission for the documents. The Commission eventually granted access to the documents. In another transparency case, Corporate Europe Observatory lodged a complaint against the Commission concerning the blanking out of the names of industrial lobbyists in documents released by the Commission. I criticised this as a breach of European transparency rules.

When the Commission launched its Green Paper on the Transparency Initiative, I made the point that its planned revision of the regulation on access to documents would represent a key test for it to show how serious it really is in this respect. On 30 April 2008, as part of the Transparency Initiative, the Commission presented a proposal for a regulation which, if finally adopted, will revise and replace Regulation 1049/2001. On 2 June, I informed the European Parliament's Civil Liberties, Justice and Home Affairs Committee of my initial views as regards the proposal. While the proposal does have certain positive aspects, which I praised in my communication to Parliament, it also raises a number of important concerns.

Regulation 1049/2001 applies to all documents held by the relevant institution. The Commission's proposal, however, introduces a new definition of "document". This proposed change implies that the rules on access would only cover those documents which have been "formally transmitted to one or more recipients" or otherwise registered. By denying that a document is a "document" until it has been formally transmitted or registered, the Commission would, for example, deny public access to documents which are circulated informally, such as documents informally passed on to favoured lobbyists. My fear is that this definition would end up reinforcing what many perceive to be an excessively secretive lobbying Brussels culture.

I have called on the European Parliament actively to use its role as co-legislator to ensure a successful reform of the current rules. The adoption of Regulation 1049/2001 by the EU legislator has greatly facilitated the process of ensuring greater openness in the Union. It is important, that, for the future, this momentum towards greater and greater openness be maintained.

Facilitating Participation in the Policy-Making Process

Greater transparency in the EU, in the form of greater access to information and more open decision-making procedures, is key to facilitating participation in the EU policy-making process. The Ombudsman has a part to play in helping to facilitate participation in the policy-making process not only by encouraging greater transparency, but also by ensuring fair and effective consultation procedures.

The growth in the lobbying industry in Brussels reflects the fact that legislation adopted here seriously affects businesses, organisations and individuals throughout the Union and beyond. The Ombudsman cannot annul legislation, nor is it my role to investigate how the political process has operated. I can, however, look into whether the Commission, in particular, has followed procedural requirements, such as the duty to carry out consultations before proposing legislation. For example, I received a complaint from the worldwide GSM Association about the EU's regulation on roaming fees. The Association alleged that the Commission abused procedures in rushing through the legislation.

A key component of the Transparency Initiative involves promoting more transparency in the activities of lobby groups at the EU level. A number of stakeholders have suggested a role for the Ombudsman in, for example, monitoring the recently introduced lobbying registration regime or in policing the code of conduct for lobbyists.

My mandate is limited to the EU public administration. Even there, I do not investigate individual wrongdoing, such as corruption, fraud or harassment. That is the role of the EU institutions themselves and of a specialised body, the European Anti-Fraud Office (OLAF). As Ombudsman, I can inquire into whether the institutions and OLAF have carried out their functions properly and whether their administrative systems are fit for purpose, including in the area of lobbying. The Treaty does not, however, give the Ombudsman any power to investigate the activities of private bodies such as interest groups, or lobbyists. This is not part of the normal role of an Ombudsman.

The Right to Good Administration

Although I cannot investigate lobbyists, I can investigate the response of "the lobbied". The European Code of Good Administrative Behaviour is key in this regard. Adopted by the European Parliament in 2001, the Code sets out the principles that the staff of the institutions and bodies should respect in their dealings with the public. The Code is addressed to the staff of the Community institutions and bodies. It contains all the principles of good administrative behaviour which they should respect in their administrative relations with the general public.

Indirectly, the Code is also addressed to public affairs practitioners – not by imposing obligations, but by setting out their rights *vis-à-vis* the EU institutions and bodies. To begin with, it contains the classic principles of administrative law, such as the principle of non-discrimination, the right to be heard and to make statements and the indication of the possibilities of appeal. It also contains provisions safeguarding greater transparency. These provisions state, for instance, that officials shall be service-minded and accessible in their relations with the public and that, when replying to correspondence, they shall try to be as helpful as possible and shall reply as completely and accurately as possible to questions which are asked. As regards requests for information, the Code requires officials to provide the public with the information that they request in a clear and understandable way.

I make extensive use of the Code of Good Administrative Behaviour in my work. The Code contributes to transparency by setting the standards for the institutions in their contacts with individuals, who in turn know what they should expect from the administration. And, correctly applied, the individual provisions of the Code make the administration much more accessible.

This Code contains principles of good administrative behaviour rather than ethical guidelines. However, applying the principles of good administration as such helps combat corruption and other inappropriate behaviour by public officials. Adhering to the principles of good administration involves establishing and following clear rules and principles about how civil servants should behave, including rules on how to handle conflicts and potential conflicts of interest. Such clear rules and principles help avoid confusion – both for the civil servants themselves and for people who are in contact with them – about what is legitimate and what is not. Confusion in this regard could have a potentially corrosive effect on personal standards of behaviour.

I have suggested that a natural complement to the European Transparency Initiative would be an initiative to ensure that all EU institutions, bodies, offices and agencies are subject to a uniform set of principles, such as those set out in the European Code of Good Administrative Behaviour. Rules on good administrative behaviour uniformly applicable to all EU bodies would not only help raise the notion of good administration to a higher level, but would also further promote transparency. In this regard, I am particularly pleased that all the EU agencies recently agreed to adopt the European Code and to consider how best to publicise it. This is good news for anyone who has reason to contact the agencies. There should now be a clear idea of what you have the right to expect.

Conclusion

To conclude, the Ombudsman was established to help improve relations between the Union institutions and the individuals, companies and associations they are in contact with. By helping to resolve complaints that are brought to his attention, and by promoting best practice, the Ombudsman aims to ensure that dealings with the EU institutions are as problem-free as possible.

In handling these cases, I consistently encourage the EU institutions not to adopt a defensive attitude to complaints. The procedures I use for inquiries give the Institution an opportunity to review and explain its position, and to put any errors right at the earliest possible stage, thereby raising the quality of its performance and its relationship with citizens. To give an example, I now include "star cases" in my Annual Report to draw attention to cases which should serve as a model for other institutions of how best to react to complaints.

By encouraging greater transparency, ensuring fair and effective consultation procedures and promoting high standards of administration, the Ombudsman can ensure that the public administration is well placed to listen to, accommodate and involve European affairs practitioners. As far as practitioners are concerned, it is important that where the EU institutions fail to respect the relevant rules or where their practices fall short, you bring this to my attention through the complaints procedure. I am here to listen – and to act.

Originally delivered as a speech to a conference organised by the Society of European Affairs Professionals on 'The European Transparency Initiative and Ethics in Lobbying' in November 2008.

The Future of Public Trust

8. *Building Trust with the EU Citizen: Is Anyone Listening?*

José Lalloum

The European Commission has for a long time made tenacious attempts to communicate with the EU citizen, with limited results. In all fairness, it has not been helped in this mission by Member States who have often used the European project as a scapegoat, praising it for certain successful initiatives but blaming "Brussels" when this helped justify domestic difficulties.

With the European Transparency Initiative, the Commission is hoping to seize an opportunity to go just one step further than its attempts to communicate: the initiative could provide an opportunity to build trust with the citizen; indeed it could form the basis for a reputation building exercise in which the roles and interactions between the EU institutions and the EU citizen are clarified. But is the citizen listening? Or have perceptions, public opinion and expectations been built and whipped through NGO campaigns which hardly ever crossed the boundaries of our public affairs microcosm?

The European Transparency Initiative deals with three aspects: transparency of EU funding, improving the way the Commission consults interested parties, and its relationship with interest representatives.

Building trust with citizens could indeed start with transparency regarding the allocation of EU funds. After all, the Commission is still in trauma as a result of the biggest scandal that shook "Brussels" and brought the Santer Commission down, when a Commissioner allocated Commission funds in a questionable manner to a friend. So it was particularly important for the Commission to address this aspect. Improving the way the Commission consults interested parties is also of particular relevance, since it needs input from experts in the field in order to feed its reflection on its legislative or policy proposals. The Commission occasionally shows signs of immaturity in this field: ask those interested parties who have been summoned to Brussels to be consulted on a complex issue with only 10 days notice...

But these two issues are only dealt with by the European Commission as a very small part of the European Transparency Initiative. The largest part of the text does not deal with the way the Commission operates, it deals with "others", i.e. interest representatives. And the register of lobbyists has attracted much more attention than the allocation of Commission funds or the way interested parties are consulted.

Do we, European public affairs consultancies have an issue with transparency? On the contrary. We consider that transparency in our dealings with the European institutions is our license to operate. We were the first group to have developed and refined a code of conduct, which has served as a model for the European Parliament's own code. We have even taken the code a step further by forming a Professional Practice Panel, composed of wise men whose role is to judge cases of complaints brought before the European Public Affairs Consultancies' Association (EPACA).

So why is the debate focusing on consultants? For our opponents, there is an obvious attraction to the sexy story of "hired guns" fighting to influence a political process for the benefit of organisations who can afford them. This angle would indeed be newsworthy. This had led me to clarify matters at the start of my mandate as Chairman of EPACA: "There is a difference between transparency and voyeurism!". As a matter of fact, financial disclosure aspects potentially have a high impact on commercial operators, such as consultants, in a different way to corporate offices or NGOs. If financial disclosure means making public the commercial agreement between my consultancy and my client, then I am being requested to disclose commercially sensitive information, an act which would often breach confidentiality agreements, and which would most certainly be to the benefit of competitors who may have chosen not to register. In fact, because of the voluntary nature of the register, it is not clear yet if I have more to lose in registering or in not registering. As the Commission wishes to attract public affairs consultants to its register, it had to take steps to protect the commercially sensitive nature of the information it asks registrants to disclose. Or make the system mandatory.

EPACA have never been afraid of the possibility of the system becoming mandatory. We have argued that, if the Commission wanted to include precise financial disclosure information to the register, it had to make it mandatory. As a result, we now have a system which provides enough information to satisfy transparency requirements, whilst protecting the main part of commercially sensitive information, through the use of bands, or ranges of 10% of turnover. Not an ideal solution for consultants. However, the fierce, aggressive reaction of our opponents to this system has been an eye-opener for the European Commission: it became clear that the "transparency" groups will never be satisfied.

A small number within our profession have questioned a discriminating treatment of and requirements from public affairs consultants which is imposed on no other profession. Let's not lament ourselves as victims of such a process. The attempt to regulate our profession is a tribute to the special role we are playing in our democracy. Transparency is our license to operate: we agree to see transparency as our objective. Then, as usual with legislation, the question is how, and how to make the system workable.

Finally, the notion that "money equals influence" with which the Commission and NGOs have been playing, is a very dangerous one, and one on which the potential effect on citizens has not been properly considered. This notion is simply false on the Brussels scene. Of course you would be better served with an experienced public affairs consultant than without. This has a price, but this price is the smallest fraction of what lobbying activities actually represent in time, effort, expertise, man-hours and budget. This notion is comparable with the idea that there may be good lobbyists and bad lobbyists – basically those who wish to save the planet, and the others. This black and white view is dated, to say the least. In the 21st century, successful interest groups and organisations have formed a societal consciousness, and are formulating their commitment on environmental and social grounds, often in partnership with NGOs.

We have entered the era of sustainable lobbying, where our actions are defined with a long-term vision. As consultants, we aim to help the legislator strike the right balance between various interests, and build Europe in a consensual way. Our role is also to help our clients build solid working relationships with those who play an active role in shaping the law, by bringing solutions to the legislator. Those who have worked with me on the consultancy side – clients, colleagues, legislators, stakeholders – will know that my approach is to first measure the possibility of complying, or striking a deal, instead of rushing headlong into lobbying operations.

Lobbying has a political price. When the decision is made to campaign, consensus is still the name of the game: this is the idea behind sustainable lobbying. One does not obtain lasting effects by sabotaging or abusing the process. From that point of view, consultancies have a role to play in guaranteeing that their clients play openly, build a reputation in the long run, which will benefit both the client and its advisor.

So what should we make of the European Commission's register? It is of course not perfect, the definitions and guidelines are not precise, and there is still room for improvement. The answer is nevertheless: register, of course. With all its imperfection, the register is a step in the right direction. Any substantial change to the register will need to be achieved through a piece of legislation, under co-decision. This will take time. Expectations have been raised for now, and the responsible answer is to register voluntarily.

There are in addition a number of ethical aspects which are not covered by the European Commission's register. Our profession's self-disciplinary processes will therefore continue to play a role alongside the Commission's voluntary register. This is why we have invited more wise men and women to add to the quality of our Professional Practice Panel. This is also why interest in the European Public Affairs Consultancies' Association remains high, as illustrated by our growing membership.

Our communication lines are open with the Commission, and the European Parliament, to make the ETI both robust, and workable for consultancies and other interest representatives. Our profession, through the European Public Affairs Consultancies' Association, will pursue its constructive approach on this issue. The value of lobbyists and lobbying has consistently been underlined throughout this debate. We want this notion to cross the boundaries of the "Brussels" microcosm, to reach the EU citizens. European institutions should remain open, and the diversity of interest groups' input should be facilitated. In the end, decision-makers will make their own informed choice on the basis of information at their disposal, information which operators will have to validate and make relevant to ensure that the dialogue between the legislator and interest representatives responds to the notion of sustainable lobbying.

9. *The European Transparency Initiative – Barking Up the Wrong Tree?*

Irina Michalowitz

Lobbying is often regarded as a non-transparent and therefore threatening profession by politicians and the public alike. The European Transparency Initiative's (ETI) aim is to shed more light on what EU lobbyists do and who they do it for. The ETI does propose a number of measures to tackle these issues. Some are likely to improve the situation, all of them however need more refinement. While the overall aim is to be welcomed, much has still to be done to arrive at a solution that really helps solve the problems of the relationship between EU policy-makers and lobbyists.

Four aspects need to be addressed in particular: the definition of lobbying, the treatment of the Initiative's target groups, the voluntary character of the Initiative's core element – a register for lobbyists – and, most importantly, the adequacy of the Initiative's purpose. The following comments critically assess these four aspects and seek to point out directions into which a useful transparency initiative should develop.

Defining Lobbying

The key to all measures of the ETI is the definition of lobbying, as only activities under the scope of lobbying are to be covered by the initiative's proposed measures. This is especially important with regard to the question of what will fall under the scope of the declaration of financial resources.

Most interest representatives carry out a variety of activities of which some are directly important for lobbying, some indirectly, and some not at all. Most of the daily work of a lobbyist consists of policy monitoring and the gathering of information in order to understand the political context of decision-making processes. Lobbyists predominantly gather information and try to explain their understanding of the policy process to their employers and the situation of their employers to policy-makers. Most interest representatives would consider only about 10% of their work as direct lobbying in the strictest sense[1]. Think tanks would even consider 0%

---

1. Strauch, M. (1993) Lobbying: *Wirtschaft und Politik im Wechselspiel*, Frankfurt: FAZ. Also see Spencer, T. (2006) "Analysis: The European Transparency Initiative Green Paper – Assessing the Evidence", available at <http://www.euractiv.com/29/images/SpencerTransparencyInitiative_tcm29-157730.pdf>.

of their work aimed at exerting direct influence, although they are aiming at indirectly shaping the agenda and debate within the EU institutions – and thereby influence EU politics. Consultancies are likely to declare far less of their work as direct lobbying because they generally act as contact and information brokers and give strategic advice to their clients. Only rarely do they carry out the actual lobbying. Of course their work is likely to amount to influence of their clients on policy issues – but strictly speaking, they would not have to declare these tasks as lobbying, especially when applying the definition of the ETI Green Paper.

The Green Paper defines lobbying very broadly as "all activities carried out with the objective of influencing the policy formulation and decision-making processes of the European institutions". This definition leaves much room for interpretation as to what interest representatives are to declare – and for which they should reveal the financial background. The idea as such may be useful because it helps understand what lobbyists are paid for.

However, the ETI definition of lobbying is not sufficiently accurate for a useful application to interest representatives. How much, and what exactly is lobbying? Is it already the analysis of documents, or only the active approach? If so, what has to be declared? Actors will seek to declare as little as possible, so nothing is gained by leaving them room for interpretation. At the same time, it may not be important to know about all financial resources of various lobbying actor types. For reasons of administrative simplicity, the register should certainly not require more revelations than are actually useful. This has to be refined, in order to come to satisfactory information about all activities linked to lobbying outcomes while maintaining the commensurability of the measure.

The ETI's Target Groups

The ETI essentially targets four groups of actors: company representatives, consultancies, non-governmental organisations (NGOs) and think tanks. With these groups, the ETI has chosen a fairly encompassing approach and succeeds in including the major actors of lobbying in Brussels. It also seeks to take into account the different tasks of these lobbyists. NGOs often have interest representation as their major purpose, the work of think tanks is also in its entirety geared towards knowledge development which may constitute lobbying. Company representatives generally constitute or take part in a corporate communication or regulatory affairs department and may have complementary tasks. Public affairs consultancies may carry out a whole variety of tasks of which activities connected to lobbying only constitute a minor part.

Hence, the Commission seeks to treat the groups differently. And this is where the problem begins. Professional consultancies will be required to reveal the turnover linked to lobbying EU institutions and the relative weight of the clients in this turnover. This will only constitute a small amount of the overall tasks of consultancies, albeit these tasks will primarily enable the clients to influence EU policy. In-house lobbyists and trade associations will have to reveal an estimate of the costs associated with direct lobbying. This will not reveal much information about the actual influence of either companies or associations. Declaring financial interests are usually of no big problem for those whose interests are relatively clear and whose tasks clearly relate to lobbying, i.e. company in-house offices and interest groups. However, what is won when receiving in writing that these offices are financed by their respective members or companies? Notably, this does not give any information about their influence. In-house lobbyists primarily exert indirect influence, via taking up important positions within their associations and driving the positions of these interest groups; time and engagement is the resource, not the money.

The only group to reveal their overall budget is the group of NGOs and think tanks. They will be required to reveal the overall budget and main sources of funding, such as the amounts and sources of public funding, donations and membership fees. This requirement is astonishing; especially as the information about EU funding – the sum the Commission is especially interested in because of the reproach of financial dependency of NGOs – can be easily gathered without a voluntary register since these declarations have to be made by NGOs when applying for funding already. What the Commission rather seeks to know here is which of the NGOs (or think tanks) that it finances for various purposes are also carrying out lobbying activities. That is a legitimate interest – and it could have serious consequences for NGOs. Such consequences would be surprising however, because NGOs, especially the ones created by the Commission, rightly or wrongly, are certainly least reproached of distorting political decision-making in an immoral way.

For think tanks, the situation is a bit different because information about whether or not a think tank is an independent institution or one with a certain political or economic interest is important to know when using the output of this think tank. However, especially the think tanks themselves refuse to be named lobbyists, and indeed, their work differs. The differential treatment is clearly stricter for NGOs and for think tanks than for any other actor under the scope of the initiative.

However, none of this information will help avoid false information or overlobbying. The financial dependency of NGOs can only be decreased if these NGOs receive less funding – which will most likely result in their disappearance, which does not seem to be in the interest of the Commission either, if it explicitly creates such groups in the first place. This is evident when looking at the financial resources made available for civil society organisations in the funding programmes, for instance, of the Directorates General Environment, Research, Employment or Health & Consumer Protection. Information on whether there actually is an imbalance in financing between NGOs and business would be very interesting as there are no existing statistics on that. But then, we need full disclosure. In any case, that is beside the point as well because the knowledge will not change the relationship of policy-makers and lobbyists – no matter who has more funds, the expertise is needed. Already, policy-makers prefer speaking to business than to NGOs, because this is where they receive the technical information needed to make a legislative act work.

Voluntary Instead of Mandatory Register

A further caveat concerns the character of the planned register for lobbyists. To make compliance with the ETI more attractive, the Commission seeks an incentive-based rather than a regulation-based approach and seeks to establish a voluntary register of lobbyists. Lobbyists are required to declare their financial background and the issues they primarily work on, and they will receive preferential information and invitations to stakeholder meetings in return. This is certainly very attractive – but it will have less impact on those the Commission is really interested in: public affairs consultancies whose interests are not always obvious. Most lobbyists in Brussels will have no problem with registering themselves. The interests of specific companies, trade associations, business or public interest groups are fairly clear to everybody. Those who do not wish to declare their interests will choose not to join the register – but given the informal information channels Brussels possesses, it is unlikely that this choice will prevent them from gaining the preferential information of their fellow registered lobbyists, or yield them less influence because they may miss important stakeholder meetings. The Commission will certainly continue to include the most relevant stakeholders, irrespective of their registration in the lobby register.

Instead, the register will lead to even closer relationships between interest representatives and the Commission, because in return for the registration, the Commission seeks to disclose even more information on consultations and pre-information.

There is a group of lobbyists where the financial background and interest declaration would be helpful and even important: public affairs and legal consultancies who are conducting lobbying activities for a large number of diverse clients. However, this is the group that is least likely to register in a voluntary register – not necessarily because they have something to hide, but because they are restrained by their clients. Also, they will have greater problems than the other groups to even define which of their activities are lobbying activities. Only a mandatory register would force these lobbyists to reveal their information. It would need to be designed carefully however, in order to enable the consultancies to come to an agreement with their clients.

The ETI's Overall Purpose

Finally, the most fundamental issue of the ETI needs to be addressed – the adequacy of the ETI's overall purpose. All proposals for refinement tackled above presuppose that the ETI as such is an effective and useful initiative. However, policy-makers, the public and lobbyists must be aware of the fact that the ETI only treats the symptoms, it is not a cure for problematic relations between lobbyists and policy-makers. The ETI rests on two basic assumptions. Firstly, lobbying is expected to create a lack of transparency, and this lack of transparency is considered a threat to the legitimacy of political decision-making. Secondly, more transparency in lobbying, notably through creating more accountability of lobbyists with a code of conduct and the revelation of their financial background, is expected to solve the problem. These assumptions fail to take the greater context of EU policy-making into account.

Lobbying is largely considered a greedy, secret, sometimes illegal activity. The media – as well as regular cases of corruption facilitated by lobbyists – support this view. At the same time however, policy-makers need the contact to European and national non-governmental organisations such as Greenpeace, Amnesty International, Oxfam or ATTAC, trade associations such the Committee of Professional Agricultural Organisations in the European Union (COPA)/General Confederation of Agricultural Co-operatives in the European Union (COGECA), business interest groups such as the Mouvement des Entreprises de France (MEDEF) or the various *ad hoc* or more formalised citizen initiatives in order to understand the problems of the individual citizen and to decide accordingly. All these mediators of information are lobbyists too. The interest of policy-makers is therefore not to create obstacles for lobbyists, but to stop those who do perform their activities in an illegal way and who may thereby harm the democratic and pluralist debate in political processes. By putting the issue of financial resources in the spotlight instead, and despite a declaration supporting the importance of lobbying in the Green Paper on the ETI itself, the Commission has unfortunately put oil into the fire of lobby-scepticism and has re-triggered a lot of discussion over lobbying as a negative component of political decision-making. That is not helpful to either side and the overall focus is not helping to solve the problems the Commission identified in its relationship to lobbyists.

The crucial problem at the European level is that policy-makers themselves do not possess a strong mandate by the EU citizens. The European Commission as the strongest European institution is a bureaucratic body whose members are European civil servants, selected on the basis of their performance in the so-called *concours* (the entry exams for a career in the European Commission), hired for a limited amount of time, or they are sent by national public bodies as so-called "national experts". The Commissioners and the Commission President are appointed by the national governments and approved by the European Parliament. The Council of the European Union as the body with the final decision-making power consists of national ministers; the European Council consists of the Heads of State. These individuals possess an indirect mandate for European decision-making, as they have been elected on the Member State level, essentially for their work at the national level – but the office also gives them the power to act on behalf of the citizens of their member state at the European and international level. Many citizens do not realise the scope of the vote they cast in national elections and are therefore not aware of the positions they agreed to support by this vote. The European Parliament is the only directly elected European institution. Its powers have substantially increased from a very weak institution to an important element of the European checks and balances. However, it still lacks the right to initiate legislation, which hinders it to develop a political agenda of European policy-making of its own.

These weaknesses lead to a distance between European institutions and EU citizens. Lobbyists are viewed as a group of representatives of these citizens that can help decrease the distance and hence strengthen the legitimacy of the decisions of the weakly legitimated EU institutions, because a large number of public and private stakeholders seek to represent their particular interests at the EU level. This is expressed in initiatives such as the White Paper on European governance, where an increased participation of organised civil society is explicitly desired.

The real problem is that first, nobody knows to what extent policy-makers make decisions based on their own conviction, and to what extent special interests make decisions that are merely signed by policy-makers. Second, that lobbyists are used to substitute the formal mandate EU institutions should receive by the citizens to gain democratic legitimation for their output. If policy-makers indeed consider lobbyists such a crucial factor in decision-making, we face an additional problem by the fact that no information exists on whether the included lobbyists really represent all stakeholders – and if, even if this information is around, they are actually included. Many High-Level Groups of the Commission only seek members who can contribute factual knowledge on the technical issue because the Commission officials in charge believe that the political debate only commences at the Parliamentary level. In these cases, NGOs, for instance, are not even invited. This information would have to exceed the knowledge a broad register can provide. It would be needed on the basis of each and every policy process.

What Will Happen and What Should Happen?

Despite the above criticism, the ETI also has a number of good points. Of course lobbyists do not always stick to the rules of respectful interaction, and some stakeholders may seek to pressure in ways that do require stronger regulation. According to the ETI, four issues are especially annoying. These are the dissemination of false or rather, clearly imbalanced information and pressurising via tools such as email spamming. Additionally, the Commission understands that there is a dilemma in their relationship to NGOs. The Commission has created many of them in order to obtain a balanced view on policy issues, and the Commission continues to see the imbalance of financial resources in interest representation between business and public interests as a problem. It lacks however the figures to understand how large this imbalance actually is and therefore the basis for any action. Many of the NGOs in Brussels rely on the financing of the Commission. This dependency is a crucial problem because it creates a conflict of interests for NGOs as well as for the Commission. Finally, each policy-maker should have the right to clearly understand on whose behalf a lobbyist is speaking. Consequently, the ETI stresses that the "the main objective of revealing how interest representatives are funded is to ensure that decision-makers and the general public can identify and assess the strength of the most important driving forces behind a given lobbying activity".

Knowing more about the number of lobbyists, their distribution over the issues lobbied and the budget spent on lobbying activities, even if ill-defined and only suitable as an indicator covering activities directly related to lobbying in a strict sense is interesting and gives an idea on what it costs to be involved at EU level. Perhaps it will also raise the awareness of policy-makers for the need of a balance between the voices of those who can afford a professional representation and those who cannot, and are therefore not as present as those with lobbyists.

However, the tools of the ETI are largely inadequate to achieve its purpose. The greater transparency, especially with regard to the financial resources of lobbyists, will serve to satisfy public interest and may facilitate to shift the blame for political decisions to a greater or smaller degree to lobbying efforts. Those who lobby over-aggressively will continue to do so however, normally because they do not know any better, because they are forced to by their members or clients, or for other reasons. They may use other means than those forbidden by a code of conduct, but the problem will not go away. False or distorted information will not cease either. Experienced lobbyists know very well that their information needs to be correct, because a politician who was once falsely informed and used that information will never trust this lobbyist again and will ensure that fellow decision-makers are made aware of the situation as well. In economic terms, those who give false information are sorted out by the market, and they are easy to detect. Of course every lobbyist will interpret information from their point of view. From a neutral standpoint, this is already distortion, but it is also a lobbyist's job. For this reason, politicians should certainly know who they are talking to and on whose behalf the lobbyists speak – but this is essentially transparent already, the planned register will not change that situation and certainly not prevent false information.

Financial dependencies will also continue – because particularly the European Commission has a clear interest in creating NGOs, and hence in the co-operation with them. Apart from the fact that Commission-financed NGOs have to reveal their financial sources for project applications anyhow, the register is suited to enable a tight grip of the Commission on the positions NGOs take, because the financial information could be used to forbid them to use Commission funds for lobbying. If they do so, the basic reason for the existence of those NGOs is questioned, because the Commission's original purpose of supporting them is to create a balance of voices at the EU level. If this is a legitimate purpose of a governmental institution can be debated (such a creation of interest groups is illegal in the US, and in democratic pluralist systems such interest groups should emerge bottom-up), but the financial register is not the means to do so, and as the major new budget lines of other Commission Directorate Generals show, is also not the desired goal.

So, what should be done in order to make the ETI work? Overall, the ETI fails to realise that – other than in the US, for instance – influence in EU policy-making is far less about money spent than about informal power, networking, contacts, and how good a lobbyist is at using them. It is more important to know who lobbyists have contact with and on which issues they are working. The register will give an indication of the broad issue areas interest representatives are working on – and this is where the emphasis in the analysis should be placed and should be linked to the policy-makers with frequent contact to interest representatives. The following measures are suited to ensure that

information is obtained that can actually make lobbying more transparent and lobbyists as well as policy-makers more accountable:
- Assess by taking stock and comparing inputs to public consultations which issues interest representatives are working on;
- Make regular surveys on the interaction between policy-makers and lobbyists. Which Members of the European Parliament and which Commission officials are in contact with which interest representatives, and how often, working on which issue?;
- Regularly compare opinions given by Members of the European Parliament and Commission officials on particular issues and the position papers of respective interest representatives; and
- Collect participant lists of events attended by policy-makers as speakers. This is important because when policy-makers are invited as speakers, they are henceforth lobbied by the audience. The personal contact and the question round are for many lobbyists the main purpose of these events.

These measures should not have as a consequence to restrict this contact. The mediating role of lobbyists is important in large complex political systems such as the European Union. They should however help understand who is representing whom. This would help all sides – policy-makers, the public and lobbyists who desperately seek to improve their image – to gain more transparency.

Originally written in May 2007 as an article in CERI's magazine, Kiosque. CERI is the premier French university-level centre for international political research.

10. *Registering Intelligently?: An ECPA Recommendation*

Conor McGrath

At an ECPA Management Board seminar on 9 October 2008, one session focused on the challenge for organisations of registering intelligently under the new European Transparency Initiative mechanisms. That discussion has resulted in the checklist below, which the ECPA offers as guidance to its member companies and others as they consider how best to register. We begin by raising a number of key issues which informed the discussion.

Many organisations are currently wrestling with the issue of whether and how to be included on the voluntary register of interest representatives. That register was launched on 23 June 2008, and as of 16 November 542 bodies had registered. The Commission is aware that many groups are currently considering how to register, and we can expect that by the end of this year most companies and organisations which are serious about public affairs will have registered.

Despite the fact that Siim Kallas stated when the register was launched that its operation would be reviewed after 12 months, it is more likely that no substantive move in this direction will be made until towards the end of 2009 – strict adherence to the 12 month schedule would be nonsensical given the imminent Parliament elections and establishment of a new team of Commissioners.

We must deal with life as it presents itself now, though, and at the minute organisations are being urged to voluntarily sign up to a register and a process which seem to be deliberately vague in important respects. The Commission apparently intends to "learn as it goes", but what does that mean? As things stand, it will be difficult if not impossible for safe assumptions to be made on the basis of the information registered, since the Commission does not provide for the use of a single, clear, calculation method. That is not to say, though, that some will not attempt to use the registrations to make unsafe assumptions. For that reason, all those in public affairs will benefit from a coherent approach to registration, at least coherence within each industry or sector – if, for example, one car company registers only its spending in Brussels while another declares all its expenditure across the EU and a third registers its global spending, they will appear to be vastly different organisations. It is important that registrations are completed in some rational manner because this is fundamentally a political process and there is no doubt that the registrations will be subject to intense media and political scrutiny.

The ECPA seminar heard from Stephen Stacey of Toyota, a company which is intending to register in the very near future. It is precisely because Toyota takes public affairs seriously that it did not rush out to sign up immediately, but rather engaged in significant internal discussion at senior management level and in external consideration of opinion within the trade associations of which it is a member. Toyota believes strongly in the value of a Code of Conduct to which lobbyists adhere; indeed, its own company Code of Conduct includes two pages on government affairs. It is also true that ETI registration presents two particular challenges which every organisation must address – first, the issue of defining lobbying (who within the company actually undertakes lobbying, and for what proportion of their time?) and, second, the vexed question of financial disclosure (how to arrive at a meaningful formula which includes as much information as possible such as fractions of salaries and internal rent for office space without unnecessarily overstating the true position).

These two issues tend – with good reason – to dominate thinking about registration by all organisations at the minute. Given that, it can be easy to lose sight of some of the positive benefits which could result from registration. Alain Perroy of Cefic reminded the seminar that while any new system can be thought of in terms of rules and burdens and bureaucracy, in fact there is a value to increased transparency. Much of what the ETI stands for is useful – most PA practitioners would love to see a greater transparency in the operation of the Council and of many NGOs, and thus it is incumbent on them to similarly welcome the ETI call for greater transparency in the whole EU policy-making process. Registration itself can be a very strong positive: instead of being pictured as shadowy figures operating behind closed doors, ETI gives practitioners a valuable opportunity to be listed publically and thus to boost the legitimacy of their work in the eyes of public opinion. Moreover, it is likely that some NGOs will have to register much higher expenditures than many companies, which may help to reposition the debate about who exercises most influence over EU policy-making.

Raj Chari (of Trinity College, Dublin) gave the ECPA seminar an insight into how the ETI system compares with different regulatory environments for lobbying, particularly in the eight nations/institutions where registration is required – the United States, Germany, Canada, the European Parliament, Lithuania, Hungary, Poland and Australia. In stark contrast to those systems, ETI registration is voluntary. Chari's research team applies a methodology based around six themes: the level of detail called for in registering; financial disclosure; whether registration is online or paper-based; public access to the information; enforcement mechanisms; and "revolving door" provisions for a cooling-off period for public officials moving into the private sector. He finds that the 42 jurisdictions which the strongest regulation are all US states plus the US federal system. With the exception of Pennsylvania (which uniquely in the US has no state lobbying regulation), all US states are either highly or medium regulated. The three nations in Central and Eastern Europe which operate lobbying regulation have a medium regulatory system, as do Canada (both at a federal level and in individual provinces) and Australia. The European Commission's new system falls, according to Chari, at the low end of the medium regulation band, while the European Parliament and Germany are classified as having low regulation. Chari's conclusion is thus that if an organisation which lobbies the Commission also lobbies in almost any of the other nations/institutions which regulate lobbying activities, then that organisation is already subject to more strict regulation in those other locations.

It is useful to have these comparisons in mind as an organisation considers the issues raised by ETI registration. They do, however, essentially measure the weight of regulation rather than the efficiency of transparency. Clearly, there is some connection between regulation and transparency, but they are not necessarily the same thing. We may intuitively believe that some relationship exists between rules and actions, but there is no direct correlation between high regulation and an absence of improper behaviour. In any event, whether operating under mandatory regulation, a self-regulatory regime or in a system which operates no formal regulation, it remains true that the first and best defence against illegitimate activity is the professional's own personal sense of ethics and integrity.

While the Commission does not apparently intend to audit the information contained in an organisation's registration, or attempt to verify its factual accuracy, nonetheless registration risks becoming meaningless (or worse – misleading) unless it provides a reasonable and fair representation of who does what and with what resources. Some organisations will find it easier than others to arrive at a very precise calculation of what proportion of their income or expenditure should be accounted for as lobbying. This is then compounded by the fact that firms in a given sector may want to apply some commonly agreed formula, to allow any comparisons made between them by others to be valid. Anecdotally it appears that many organisations are tending at the minute to more or less intuitively feel that direct lobbying of EU institutions occupies something like 20% or 25% of their total spending. Any such figure can be arrived at in a number of ways – precise calculations may be possible through which a number is arrived at, or conversely precise calculations may be undertaken to justify an already decided-upon number. Organisations will produce their own accounting using their own standards for their own reasons. The ECPA can merely suggest that if absolute precision is problematic, a reasonable estimate made in good faith for the purposes of representing an order of magnitude may be more achievable.

Other specific concerns about the registration system established under ETI are valid and ought to be acknowledged. There is among many groups a continuing nervousness around the possible impact of registration on fiscal matters, particularly the VAT status of organisations under Belgium law, and greater clarity here would be enormously welcome. There is also a need to take care over precisely what information is included in an organisation's registration and how it is presented, being aware of how such information may be used or misused by policy-makers, journalists and activists. Such scrutiny, though, can be exaggerated – registrations will initially trigger a surge of media reports but that will die down over time.

We should also keep in mind that we are merely at the beginning of a process which will evolve over time. How this system operates will be reviewed in late 2009 and while Siim Kallas has left open the possibility that registration could yet be made mandatory, that seems unlikely provided that a critical mass of organisations register voluntarily. This is a wholly political process, driven largely by a handful of politicians, and so how it develops in the future will depend entirely upon who holds a few key posts in the next Commission team. Organisations need to work in two time zones – what to do now, and what to do in 2009 and beyond.

The sensible course of action is thus to do no harm now and register intelligently, but to do so leaving no hostages to fortune for next year. It could well be that the Commission will want something rather different by the end of its review – perhaps it will by then have concluded that money is not the best guide to influence and that instead it would be more relevant to have a declaration of who has been lobbied by whom and on whose behalf, but without requiring any breakdown of expenditure. Such a register may prove in time to be defensible politically, pragmatic for the profession and more useful to the Commission.

It is with the foregoing issues and debates in mind that the European Centre for Public Affairs offers colleagues the following checklist of questions which they may wish to reflect upon before producing their organisation's registration material.

ECPA Checklist for ETI Registration

Calculation
- What geographical base have we chosen to report on?
- Have we checked with the Commission Guidance which PA and PR expenditures should be included?
- What percentage of our total public affairs expenditure have we defined as direct lobbying activities?
- Do we anticipate a substantial difference between our submission for this year and next year? If so, why?

Internal preparation
- How much do we need to brief senior management re their involvement once we are registered?
- Are there different attitudes towards Transparency in different subsidiaries and sectors of the company?
- Have we talked to our offices in national capitals about lobbying activities designed to influence decision-making at European level?
- Have we shared our submission with all our employees involved in Comitology?
- Is our draft submission compatible with submissions made under other jurisdictions?
- Is it compatible with statements made in the context of Corporate Social Responsibility and the Global Reporting Initiative?

- Are we registered in the European Parliament Register of Lobbyists?
- Have the internal lawyers had a look at our submission?
- Have we considered the tax or VAT implications of our registration?
- Do we have a communications response ready if the details of our submission are challenged by transparency campaigners?
- Is there value in formulating a corporate statement on our attitude to Transparency above and beyond our entry in the Register?
- Do we have a corporate policy on how we want the ETI to develop under the next Commission?
- Do we support a "one-stop shop" register covering all the EU Institutions?
- Does the Commission Code of Conduct cause us any problems?

Comparison with competitors
- Have any of our direct competitors registered yet?
- Are we comfortable that the definitions and disclosures which they have offered are equivalent to our own?
- Has our Trade Association registered?
- Has our Trade Association been proactive in raising discussion of this subject?
- Have we reached agreement with our Trade Association on avoiding double counting of our membership fees, etc?

Stakeholders
- Have we explained our position to relevant stakeholders?
- Have our stakeholders registered yet?

Consultants/Lawyers
- Have we shared our views with our consultants/external lawyers?
- Do our views on registration agree with theirs?
- Have we reached agreement on double counting?

Think Tanks & Networks
- Have the think tanks which we support registered?
- Commission guidance refers to "Any Associations/Federations or other type of networks which they belong to in the EU or the world". Have we done an audit of relevant organisations?

Part II. PUBLIC AFFAIRS BEST PRACTICE

1. *Hiring Public Affairs Consultants*
Summary of Recommendations from an ECPA Working Group

This paper sets out the steps and considerations to be taken into account when requesting proposals from public affairs agencies. The success of a project, both for the "client" and for the "agency", can often depend on how the decision to work together is taken at the outset.

For clients, we want to stress that this is only a tool to help with your decision to select the right consultant or agency. It is not a rigid process to hinder you. Adapt this tool as necessary. Use your best judgment as to which performance and mastery areas are most critical to your business.

Agencies can play a major part in the process of potential clients putting out a Request for Proposal by considering a number of issues in advance. These will be important in ensuring that the match between the agency and the client is best suited to the needs of the project.

Following a debate at an ECPA Management Board Seminar a working group composed of Erik Jonnaert (Procter & Gamble), Julia Harrison (Blueprint Partners), Teemu Lehtinen (Edelman) and Rory MacMillan (Nike) prepared an extensive document which was discussed at an ECPA Consultants Roundtable in January 2005. An equal number of consultants and clients have contributed to this document at each stage. The ECPA is grateful to Maria Laptev, Vice Chairman, Fleishman-Hillard, Brussels for her creative editorial work in producing this summary.

As a Client: How to Prepare the Process

Step 1. Define the decision-maker
PA agency selection should ideally be led by the Public Affairs manager in your company. In some cases, there won't be a PA person available. The process should then be handled by one of the key business

leaders, but it must be someone who has some understanding or experience of PA. Ideally, there would be senior manager/board involvement at the outset.

Step 2: Define your PA needs, know what you want and how to ask for it

Before selecting an agency, identify the public affairs needs you have for your project or programme. First review your own capabilities in-house and clarify where an agency could possibly add value.

Step 3: Assemble the evaluation team, decide on the assessment criteria

Ideally this process should be led by the PA manager. Identify whether you need other functions to be involved when selecting the agency. Make sure the team is appropriately assembled upfront, so that there are no issues at the back-end of the process as to who did, or did not, get to participate.

Step 4: Research and select candidates/agencies

The PA manager should be able to recommend agency options. Candidates can be generated by:

- checking with local, regional or global professional organisations;
- evaluating who seems to be doing the best PA work in Brussels or in other capitals;
- leveraging your closest relationships with stakeholders (eg in the European Commission or Parliament) to ask about the agencies they find most impressive; and
- establishing whether your candidates are a member of professional PA organisation and have signed up to a PA Code of Conduct.

Step 5: Prepare the agencies for the interview

Most agencies have capabilities presentations already prepared. However, it is when meeting with the candidates that you are able to understand the potential match with your needs, well beyond the capabilities presentation.

- **Getting to know each other.** Rather than standard credentials meetings, both sides benefit from "getting to know you" meetings.
- **Defined briefing: objectives versus activities.** The briefing should be defined in terms of the objective of the process (aims, parameters, client concerns, current priorities) rather than in terms of the mechanics (activities and tools).

- *A pitch?* Is a pitch necessary if several meetings have already taken place and you have decided in advance?
- *Equal access.* As a client, do make sure you are clear about your availability for briefings, and giving all consultancies equal access.

Step 6: Hold interview meetings with the PA agency candidates

The PA person is responsible for ensuring the interview process is clear and well defined.

- *Timing.* Unless there is a real crisis, aim to set a minimum time for the proposal to be made, and be clear of the decision timetables, particularly if the pitch is competitive. Then stick to them as much as possible.
- *Budgets.* Clear budgeting guidelines should be put forward for all Requests for Proposals. If asking for substantial amount of time and work to be invested by the agency, is there justification for paying for the proposal, particularly if original strategy and ideas are involved?

Step 7: Make the decision

Once all agencies have been interviewed, ensure that all team members participating in the evaluation process have had a chance to provide their perspective. In most cases, the team will reach consensus decision on which agency to hire.

- *Feedback loop:* There is real long term value for all concerned of a feed-back loop by informing the losers as well as the winners.

As an Agency: How to Improve the Process

Step 1: Understanding the corporate agenda

In addition to the standard "boiler plate" information about a company, it is important that the agency understands the corporate agenda for the interview. Is the client looking for an exercise in "creative thinking" or seeking a clear response to a strictly defined brief?

- Agencies need to know what keeps clients awake at night.
- What are the client's main policy, political and commercial issues?
- What are the client's key success criteria such as timing, unpacking of commercial aspects, milestones and tracking of progress?
- Both sides should clarify their expectations, communicating minimum as well as ideal goals.

Step 2: Establish how the client likes to work with consultants and sees their role
- The client should situate the brief. Ask at the outset who in the client company owns the project, who else is involved and what client resources are available for the project?
- Once the project is assigned, ask the client to make clear what are the factors that an agency should take into account, such as expectations relating to information flow, benchmarking, etc.

Step 3: Getting the mechanics of the process right
- It clearly matters whether an interview is with the incumbent or with a new consultant.
- The timing of the submission of credentials and written proposals and the dates of the pitch and decision need to be made crystal clear at the beginning of the process.
- On what basis is the budgetary quote to be prepared? As a project/retainer/hour or a menu with a retainer base with services added? How are expenses covered? How do your rates compare with the market rates?
- What is the length and nature of the appointment?
- Who is the decision-maker, and who will sign off invoices? Are there other divisions involved?

Step 4: Criteria and issues arising in the selection process
- *Conflict of interest:* what is the client's conflict policy? How does it match with the agency's?
- *Confidentiality:* is there a need for a Non Disclosure Agreement?
- *People:* who is the senior manager with responsibility for the account, what is their workload, have you identified the account team working on the business, is everyone involved in the pitch going to be involved on an ongoing basis?
- *Creativity:* how do you identify risks and issues and how do you pro-actively bring them to the client?
- *Expertise:* what is the relevant expertise to this project, commercially as well as issues/Institutions/relationships?
- *Track record:* can you refer to at least two clients with whom the potential client can discuss your performance?
- *Network:* what local office affiliations exist in key countries/cities with senior management local-expertise and locally seasoned account teams?

- *Measurement:* what sort of programme evaluation or self-evaluation do you share with the client?

Step 5: Agencies appreciate additional information about the client
- Where does PA fall within the organisation?
- How does it link with Corporate Communications, legal etc?
- Is the Board involved in endorsement, driving and reporting?
- Are there other consultants on the case or in related areas?
- Ask up-front for areas of difficulty to be made clear (e.g. potential need to reduce or increase the resource at short notice).

The Future of Public Trust

2. Trade Associations and Their Corporate Members
Summary of Recommendations from an ECPA Working Group

This paper offers checklists that we hope will be of use in improving the relationship between Trade Associations and their Corporate Members.

In February 2007 the ECPA brought together a group of senior Trade Association Executives and senior Corporate public affairs figures to establish the questions they might want to ask of each other. Eric Vaes and Maria Laptev agreed to act as Rapporteurs for the process. In May 2007 a meeting of trade association executives commented on the first draft of the text. On 1st June a group of corporate practitioners and consultants further developed the text. The Rapporteurs circulated a document entitled "Best Practice Notes on Relations between Trade Associations & Their Corporate Members" on 6th June. This note was discussed at the ECPA Management Board Seminar in October. Three trade associations experimented with the texts and the creation of audits for both themselves and their corporate members.

The ECPA is grateful to the following for their many and various contributions to the text: Erik Jonnaert (Procter & Gamble), Roland-Jan Meijer, (Holcim), Ruth Rawling, (Cargill), Truus Huisman (Unilever), Tangui van der Elst (InBev), Michiel Reerink (Imperial Tobacco), Michelle O'Neil (Honeywell Europe), Martina Bianchini (Dow), Guido Kayaert (Nestlé), Hans Mattaar (Pappas & Associates), Maja Wessels (formerly Honeywell Europe), Jacqueline Smithson (Imperial Tobacco), Michael Burrell (Edelman), Jere Sullivan (Edelman), Natalie Todd (Ogilvy Public Relations Worldwide), Alain Perroy (CEFIC), Bertil Heerink (COLIPA), Johan Vanhemelrijck (Europabio), Peter van den Driest (ESTA), Susanne Zänker (AISE), Ivan Hodac (ACEA), Kai Lucke (Bosch), Alain Galaski (AIM), Oliver Gray (EASA), Adrian Harris (Orgalime), Susan Danger (AmCham EU), Stephan Loerke (WFA), Julian Carroll (Europen), Jamie Fortescue (European Spirits), Julian Lageard (INTEL), Hubert David (Eurima), and Pierre Wiertz (Edana).

Checklist for Trade Associations

A. Prioritisation

Effective mechanisms for prioritisation and the avoidance of duplication are the key building blocks in relationships between trade associations and their corporate members.
- Do we have a three year Strategic Review?
- Do we have an Annual Checklist used to review the detail of the relationship and shared priorities between us and our corporate members?
- Could we make use of a system of "variable geometry"? Should there be a minimum number of members needed for associations to deal with an issue as a priority (positioning, lobbying, etc)? Do we have a system of financing appropriate to such additional projects?
- Should we have a Sunset Clause for all committees, such that only a positive decision could lead to the continuation of a committee beyond a "natural" two year life?
- Should we have an Annual Review of the synergy between national and European levels to ensure that the best working relationship is maintained?
- Would shared training help mutual understanding?

B. Human Resourcing

- We accept the need to further professionalise performance in both corporations and trade associations. We recognise that there were generational differences on both sides in this matter.
- Have we reviewed our job descriptions to ensure their relevance for current conditions with particular attention to succession planning and career development?
- Do our young professionals need to balance their technical excellence with actual experience in companies? How could we achieve this?
- Should we regularly review the role of corporate CEOs in our Association?

C. Communication

We recognise that an agreed internal communication strategy for the Association is essential to ensure successful co-ordination with our members.

- Are we happy that the effort put into the production of Annual Reports, Reviews and other communications is good value? Have we identified a specific audience for each such document?
- Can we create a "Satisfaction Survey" that is mutually beneficial, and which measures the full range of "value added" by our association? Can we create it in a simple electronic form that encourages response from our members?
- Do we regularly audit our sector's reputation with its stakeholders? Can we avoid overlap with other stakeholder consultations?

D. Transparency

We accept that there is external pressure for transparency on both us and our corporate members.
- Should we give specific attention jointly to transparency issues in working with European Institutions, NGOs and the media?
- Can we create informal mechanisms indicating the degree of a corporation's adherence to trade association policy on sensitive issues that could be mutually useful?

E. Budgets

We recognise that there is a tension between our corporate members' desire for more service and output from the association and their reluctance to pay increased membership fees or share more resources.
- Are our membership fees directly related to the value added by membership?
- Can we create an environment in which corporations under budget pressure do not seek to cut expense by reducing personnel involvement with the inevitable loss of effectiveness for both the corporation and for our association?

Checklist for Corporate Members

A. Prioritisation

Effective mechanisms for prioritisation and the avoidance of duplication are the key building blocks in relationships between trade associations and their corporate members.
- Do we have an Annual Checklist used to review the detail of the relationship and shared priorities between us and our trade association?

- Would shared training with our trade association help mutual understanding?

B. Human Resourcing

- We accept the need to further professionalise performance in both corporations and trade associations. We recognise that there were generational differences on both sides in this matter.
- Can we contribute to the recruitment and interviewing of trade association personnel?
- How recently did we "present" ourselves to our trade association and invite trade association figures into our company for regular briefings?
- Given the variations in company and trade association structures, do we regularly review of the role of our CEO?
- Do we review annually the quality of corporate contributions to association work with attention not only to competence and attendance, but also to the levels of issue involvement and degree of connectedness inside the company?
- Should we have an annual "trade association review process" inside the company to review our deployment and share our conclusions with the trade association?
- Should our CEO annually sign off company "members" active at association level?
- Do we recognise the potential for internal competition between our divisions in certain issue areas?
- Do we recognise that the complexity of issue management and lobbying requires an improved mix of the public affairs and technical expertise assigned by corporates to trade association working groups?

C. Communication

We recognise that we need to input into the internal communication strategy for our Association.

- Do we regularly review the effectiveness of our feedback mechanisms?
- Have we agreed the structure and coverage of "assessment forms" with our trade associations?

D. Transparency

We accept that there is external pressure for transparency on both us and our trade association.

- Should we give specific attention jointly to transparency issues in working with European Institutions, NGOs and the media?
- Can we create informal mechanisms indicating the degree of our adherence to trade association policy on sensitive issues that could be mutually useful?

E. Budgets

We recognise that there is a tension between our desire for more service and output from the association and our reluctance to pay increased membership fees or share more resources.

- Are we prepared to share more details of our public affairs budgets?
- Have we made it clear to our trade association that "time is money" and that corporate budgets are tight? Have we made clear that budgetary tensions could be reduced by clear agreement on measurement of value added?

The Future of Public Trust

3. German and Austrian Public Affairs

Irina Michalowitz and Peter Köppl

Public affairs in Austria and Germany have both undergone substantial changes with similar outcomes during the past ten to 15 years which can be strongly linked to the European and global development of both public affairs and the larger context of politics. In this essay, we outline these changes and analyse the domestic as well as the European and global factors detrimental to this change. We do so by firstly outlining the *status quo*, secondly the historical background of the current state and thirdly the greater international content first for Germany, then for Austria. In our concluding section, we compare the development of public affairs in the two Germanic countries in their respective impact upon each other.

Current Position of Interest Representation in Germany

Germany's public affairs experienced a radical overhaul with the German government's move to Berlin. While public affairs was essentially left to the large, corporatist associations during the period in which the government resided in Bonn, the move to Berlin has drawn a diverse and numerous crowd of company representatives, public affairs consultancies, specialised media, associations and other actors.

Three aspects characterise the new German public affairs: political corporate communication has gained in importance, is less left to associations and is carried out with more professional methods[1]. Hence changes relate to interest representation structures as well as within these structures to the weight of different types of actors – less weight to the associations, more weight to individual company representatives (in-house lobbyists) – and the change of lobbying strategies. Companies increasingly seek to be present towards their Members of Parliament and to represent their interests individually. Medium-sized companies that cannot afford an office of their own in Berlin therefore make use of consultancies, while bigger companies are represented with liaison offices. Scholars and practitioners alike link this development to an

---

1. Busch-Janser, F. (2004) *Staat und Lobbyismus. Eine Untersuchung der Legitimation und der Instrumente unternehmerischer Einflussnahme*, Berlin/München: poli-c.books; p. 28.

increased need for advice by the political decision-makers as well as by the private actors[2].

Meanwhile, the consultancy market in Berlin has diversified and is especially characterised by four types: individual advisors with a niche expert knowledge, for instance for specific policy fields; owner-led national agencies; public affairs derivates of larger management or public affairs consultancies; and finally all-inclusive agencies with, for instance, a public relations background that offer integrated communication strategies including PR campaigns or PR strategies. Unlike the situation in other political systems, public affairs consulting is very much related to public relations in Berlin, but management consultancies and law firms are increasingly offering public affairs services as well[3].

Especially for employers' and employee interest groups, this development poses a problem. While the republic of Bonn was characterised by a manageable size of interest representations based in Bonn, 1,780 lobbyists are registered in Berlin[4]. These lobbyists are highly visible in Berlin due to the much higher amount of events, political salons and through networking as well as due to an increased media support of interest representation, which cannot be matched by the German unions and other interest representations with less resources[5]. Business associations also still have to adapt to the new situation. Here, the change of the political framework conditions led to separations of associations and newly created interest groups, linked to an increased demand of association members for professional representation and representation that is more targeted towards the respective interests' own interests. The big umbrella associations in general could not satisfy this demand[6]. Overall, German public affairs has rearranged dramatically.

2. See Kahler, T. and Lianos, M. (2003) "Neue Aktionsfelder: Agenturen in den Lobbying-Kinderschuhen", in Speth, R. and Leif, T. (eds.) *Die Stille Macht. Lobbyismus in Deutschland*, Wiesbaden: Westdeutscher Verlag, p. 292.
3. Kahler, T. and Lianos, M. (2003) "Neue Aktionsfelder: Agenturen in den Lobbying-Kinderschuhen", in Speth, R. and Leif, T. (eds.) *Die Stille Macht. Lobbyismus in Deutschland*, Wiesbaden: Westdeutscher Verlag; p. 294.
4. Klingenburg, K. (2003) "Dagegen sein ist nicht alles. Gewerkschaftliche Interessenvertretung in Berlins neuer Unübersichtlichkeit", in Leif, T. and Speth, R. (eds.) *Die Stille Macht. Lobbyismus in Deutschland*, Wiesbaden: Westdeutscher Verlag; p. 275.
5. Klingenburg, K. (2003) "Dagegen sein ist nicht alles. Gewerkschaftliche Interessenvertretung in Berlins neuer Unübersichtlichkeit", in Leif, T. and Speth, R. (eds.) *Die Stille Macht. Lobbyismus in Deutschland*, Wiesbaden: Westdeutscher Verlag; pp. 273-5.
6. Schröder, W. (2003) "Lobby pur. Unternehmerverbaende als klassische Interessenvertreter", in Leif, T. and Speth, R. (eds.) *Die Stille Macht. Lobbyismus in Deutschland*, Wiesbaden: Westdeutscher Verlag; p. 288.

Steps of Development up to the German *Status Quo*

The question is why this change happened. The mere move of the capital from the provincial Bonn to the more mundane Berlin is certainly not a sufficient explanation for the change. When looking into the German literature of interest group research, two factors appear to serve as facilitators.

First, the increasing globalisation of financial and capital markets has changed the role of the state for the well-being of Germany's larger companies. The stock exchange listing of companies who were previously part of the so-called "Germany Holding" affected the steering capacity of the German government. Germany's associations therefore do not manage any longer to guarantee an encompassing societal interest representation as representative bodies to their members[7].

Second and linked to the factor of globalisation, an increased demand for a type of interest representation has arisen that many private actors are used to from Brussels or from Washington, D.C. These two centres of public affairs already display a diversified system of collective and individual interest representation of a large variety of actors. Public affairs consultancies in Berlin often possess partnerships with consultancy firms in Brussels and/or other national capitals, large German companies have maintained offices in Brussels and/or Washington, D.C. for a long time already. The increasing dependence of national decision-making on the European level also necessitates stronger links especially to the European level, which is also likely to have had a learning effect.

German Public Affairs between International and Domestic Conditions

The arguments presented above already hint at the influential role of Europe and of the international context of German politics and public affairs. Economic Europeanisation and globalisation have in particular fostered a demand for an adaptation of public affairs to the European and American systems, which especially those players who are already active in lobbying on these levels, deem more professional. Besides individual, targeted interest representation, enterprises in Germany predominantly demand a changed communication strategy.

---

7. Streeck, W. and Höpner, M. (eds.) (2003) *Alle Macht dem Markt? Fallstudien zur Abwicklung der Deutschland AG*, Frankfurt am Main: Campus.

Due to the increased competition between interest representatives, associations also have to enlarge the diversity of their methods. This firstly concerns their strategic behaviour. Agencies offer a strong expert knowledge for the political process and develop management consultancy-like strategies of campaigns for interest representation on a particular topic, their staff members possess the necessary training to do so. In-house lobbyists of companies offer interest representation that is strictly targeted at the enterprise and that does not need a prior compromise of association members. As has been observable for a long time at the European level, resource-strong enterprises in Germany therefore increasingly seek a multiple representation via different interest types in Berlin[8].

In terms of the contents, change is also expectable and in the long term even to a higher degree: what has been described as professionalisation of lobbying[9] is essentially a new approach as has been described for the European level before[10]. The typical association representative used to originate from the association itself or was a designated expert sent by one of its members whose expert knowledge was linked to the sectoral interest of the association and who had to still learn the rules of the political process and the unwritten rules of its communication. The new type of lobbyists consists of academics with a legal, political science or economic background, on the EU level quite often with a complementary degree in European studies. They know the political process and the important context and access points and mediate between political actors and association members or enterprises[11].

Some aspects do not change however. The conditions of the German political system induce characteristics of lobbying behaviour which are particular for this state. Germany possesses a system of fragmented power, characterised by a federalist structure, a multiple-party system that depends on a proportional voting system and a strong ministerial bureaucracy with the autonomy for their portfolios, countered by a strongly centralised

---

8. Busch-Janser, F. (2004) *Staat und Lobbyismus. Eine Untersuchung der Legitimation und der Instrumente unternehmerischer Einflussnahme*, Berlin/München: poli-c.books; p. 29.
9. Schröder, W. (2003) "Lobby pur. Unternehmerverbaende als klassische Interessenvertreter", in Leif, T. and Speth, R. (eds.) *Die Stille Macht. Lobbyismus in Deutschland*, Wiesbaden: Westdeutscher Verlag; pp. 281-99. Also see Busch-Janser, F. (2004) *Staat und Lobbyismus. Eine Untersuchung der Legitimation und der Instrumente unternehmerischer Einflussnahme*, Berlin/München: poli-c.books; p. 28.
10. Lahusen, C. and Jauß, C. (2001) *Lobbying als Beruf. Interessengruppen in der Europäischen Union*, Baden-Baden: Nomos.
11. Lahusen, C. and Jauß, C. (2001) *Lobbying als Beruf. Interessengruppen in der Europäischen Union*, Baden-Baden: Nomos.

system of associations[12]. This structure is complemented by strong party discipline and a dominance of the executive power over the legislative power. These conditions force German public affairs professionals to adapt to party interests and party networks more strongly than at the EU level, as the German Government and Parliament are responsible for both formal legislative initiatives and their ratification, and both are elected bodies with a corresponding strong obligation to their parties and the party members. Additionally, the interests of Germany's federal states play an impressive role and are also determined by the parties. The impact of the party positions on the success and failure of interest representation is strong and cannot be neutralised by changing communication and actor strategies.

Current Position of Public Affairs in Austria

Public Affairs in Austria also changed during the past ten to 15 years. In this country, the changes are predominantly related to the changes of the domestic political and economic conditions for Austria due to the country's accession to the EU in 1995.

Austria's former, almost exclusively corporatist system of the so-called "social partnership" has weakened. Since Austria's accession to the EU, new types of actors in the form of individualised representatives such as company in-house lobbyists and public affairs consultancies has emerged.

Company in-house lobbyists are particularly employed by former state-owned companies, for two reasons: firstly, these companies belong to the category of the largest Austrian companies and therefore possess the resources to invest more strongly in their public affairs. Secondly, the privatisation of these companies took especially place in newly emerging sectors that were liberalised Europe-wide: these new sectors are less well represented by the traditional associations in Austria.

Public affairs consultancies are the most visible group of new actors in Austrian interest representation. They consist mostly of small to medium-sized consultancy firms that formerly focussed on public relations services. Two consultancy networks connect the firms with each other and seek a professionalisation of the profession. The Public Affairs Society of

---

12. Streeck, W. and Höpner, M. (eds.) (2003) *Alle Macht dem Markt? Fallstudien zur Abwicklung der Deutschland AG*, Frankfurt am Main: Campus.

Austria (PASA) is an organisation of public affairs consultancies under the umbrella of the Public Relations Association of Austria (PRVA), and the Austrian Lobbying & Public Affairs Council (ALPAC) unites independent owners of public affairs consultancies. PASA members understand lobbying as an element of public relations and, consequently, as a means to shape political communication rather than to shape political opinions.

The Austrian Lobbying and Public Affairs Council (ALPAC) combines members who view lobbying as an activity that should be treated separately from Public Relations. ALPAC defines lobbying as the attempt to influence the contents of political decision-making. ALPAC also seeks international co-operations and maintains close relations with the German Association of Political Consultancy (DEGEPOL), the German Institute for Public Affairs (DIPA), the Swiss Association for Public Affairs, the European Public Affairs Council (ECPA) as well as the American Public Affairs Council (PAC).

Steps of Development up to the Austrian *Status Quo*

The changes described above are particularly surprising in Austria, because this country's interest representation was reserved to a number of key associations who had a very deep impact on various aspects of the political, economic and societal life – the so-called "social partners". The balance of interests in Austria's Second Republic has so far been met primarily by the *"Sozialpartnerschaft"* (social partnership), an informal body of the following four institutions: Chamber of Commerce, Chamber of Labour, Austrian Federation of Unions, and Presidential Conference of Chambers of Agriculture, all with obligatory membership. In 2008, the role, functions and membership of these associations has even been manifested by their inclusion in the Austrian constitution – which demonstrates the strong political significance and powers the social partners used to have, and to some extent are still able to exert. Decision-making was (and largely still is) co-ordinated in parallel on the levels of the national government, the federal counterparts as well as with the social partners.

The result was a highly politicised society. For instance, the political affiliation of high-ranking staff in the public service, but also in companies or private institutions has been and remains an important criterion for hiring. In the political life, very close personal relations have developed from this practice between public and private actors. These ties are crucial because Austria's politics overall displays little change in terms of the ruling parties – Austria was ruled by a Great Coalition from 1947 to 1966 and from 1987 to 2000 – and because the political elite remained a small one.

The strong personal ties can also be seen as the major reason why at least informally, the importance of the social partners has remained high even after the change of government in 2000. When the Austrian Freedom Party (FPÖ) came to power in a coalition with the conservative Austrian People's Party (ÖVP), one of its major intentions was to break up the strong corporatist political and societal culture. The governmental change forced the social partners and their members to search for additional ways to advocate their interests. Notably the larger Austrian companies realised that they needed a representation tailored specifically to their needs. This was the hour of the political consultancy businesses in Austria. The FPÖ's critical attitude, but also the increasing complexity of politics due to Austria's accession to the EU, liberalisation and globalisation, opened up a niche for agencies that were able to translate the needs and demands of companies, but also of the social partners, into the changing political language[13].

A number of political processes related to domestic factors and to Austria's role in the European Union provided an opportunity window for new public affairs actors. First, Austria's accession to the EU was linked to the obligation to adopt the rules of the European aquis communautaire. This largely decreased the power of the social partners within the Austrian enterprises. Second, the liberal-right-wing Austrian Freedom Party came to power as a coalition partner with the Austrian People's Party in 2000 and made it a declared goal to break up the corporatist structures. The change in government hence forced the social partners and their members to search for new ways of interest representation. Especially the larger Austrian enterprises realised at this point that they needed a more specialised representation tailored to their specific needs.

The changes were furthermore supported by clear political signals and the (lacking) ability of the social partners to adapt. Since 2001, a massive transformation of the system of interest representation took place which was accompanied by a visible weakening of the real political role of the

---

13. Michalowitz, I. (2006) "Österreich: ein Public-Affairs-Sektor im Entstehen", *Public Affairs Manager*, 2(1), pp. 106-18.

social partners as well as by the emergence of public affairs as a profession. Four factors were particularly instrumental. First, the Chancellor under the coalition of ÖVP and FPÖ consciously and publicly broke the tradition of permanent, institutionalised consultation of the social partners in the processes of the Austrian day-to-day politics. On the contrary, the new government rejected their influence and thereby contributed to a weakening of the tradition and of the organisation of this social partnership. Second, the Austrian Association of Industrialists *(Österreichische Industriellenvereinigung)* – a voluntary organisation of interest representation of industrial enterprises – which was not part of the social partnership, managed to use the vacuum of power to their advantage. Experienced in international lobbying due to the long-term membership in the European umbrella association "BusinessEurope" (formerly UNICE), the *Industriellenvereinigung* managed to position itself as a lobby organisation of a European dimension. The quickly-gained influence and the political successes of the *Industriellenvereinigun* weakend the social partnership even further, both symbolically as well as in terms of their actual influence. This development proved to be sustaining.

Third, the Austrian Federation of Unions *(Österreichischer Gewerkschaftsbund, ÖGB)* imploded in 2006 as a consequence of a scandal surrounding the bank BAWAG. The major share of this bank belongs to the ÖGB and is therefore the financial backbone of the union. The bank stumbled over highly risky speculations in the Caribbean and exaggerated salaries for their top managers – accepted by the Union leadership. The formerly strong social partner-organisation had to quickly concentrate on damage minimisation and a re-organisation and lost within a few months almost all of its political weight – at least in comparison with its power in the decades before. Fourth, a few months before the Austrian Parliamentary elections in 2006, the back then SPÖ party chief and now Chancellor Alfred Gusenbauer took all ÖGB officials off the list of the SPÖ Members of Parliament. To this point, the Union heads had traditionally been active as Members of Parliament, as a consequence of a political automatism. Gusenbauer's decision ended a last bastion of the social partnership. Gusenbauer has now held the office of the Austrian Chancellor for half a year. His position indicates that he will continue his predecessor's way of interacting with the social partners. This gives space for new actors to investigate new ways of interacting with political decision-makers – and can be seen as a direct cause of the boom of public affairs consultancies.

Austrian Public Affairs in a European and Global Context

The accession to the EU as a cause for a change of Austrian public affairs has already been mentioned. However, Europe influenced Austria even beyond the initial creation of an opportunity window for a pluralisation of Austrian public affairs actors. Overall, the accession to the EU and the thereby gained experience with public affairs practices at the European level, together with changed demands and needs of decision-makers and private actors alike, seem to have led to a greater acceptance of lobbying and public affairs in Austria. On the one hand, decision-makers and private actors recognise a need for a diversified and enlarged interest representation because they otherwise lack sufficient information in an increasingly complex world. On the other hand, the stronger diversification appears to also have brought about a visible pluralisation of interests, which lead to a more sensibilised and more critical approach of decision-makers when confronted with special interests. For this reason, they view lobbying positively and as an asset for their work.

Conclusions

Austrian and German public affairs are characterised by major, recent changes. These concern especially the structure of interest representation and the change of political communication. German public affairs now consists of a larger diversity of actors, but the conditions of the institutional political system in Germany remain. Consequently, associations remain powerful, even under the condition of a stronger participation of other actors of interest representation. Austria has also developed its own specific public affairs style which is linked to the societal and political conditions in the country, which is in the course of finding its role, balancing between political traditions and international necessities. A much more strategic alignment and consequently, the use of options which both political systems now offer to new actors becomes visible in both Germany and Austria. In Austria, the strong personal relations between political and economic elites will remain an enduring factor of public affairs – although this factor is often overrated, according to experts of the Viennese political life. At the same time, the more diverse and complementary choice of public affairs instruments and strategies is certainly of high interest especially for international enterprises who are used to such a choice at the international or European level. Overall, public affairs in Germany and Austria display an exciting mix of learning from the international and European contexts and adapting to domestic developments.

4. Public Affairs in Europe – The Same Everywhere or Different?

Michael Burrell

Ever since it was founded, 20 years ago, the European Centre for Public Affairs has sought both to help practitioners to understand how the European Union institutions were evolving and how public affairs best practice in national capitals required a proper understanding of national institutions and culture.

It is on that dual mission that this chapter focuses. Specifically, it seeks to examine this question: Is it the case that public affairs is essentially the same everywhere (since it deals only with one race, the human race) or is it so different in different capitals that any attempt to roll out a single model (as some, less sophisticated American companies have on occasion been accused of doing) is doomed to failure? Or does the truth lie somewhere between those two extremes?

What follows is not the result of ECPA academic research or even an opinion survey, but rather is based on personal experience and the observations of colleagues and inevitably biased by both my nationality (British/English) and the locations where I have worked (primarily London and Brussels).

It is also probably biased, to some degree, by the time of writing – in the shadow of the global credit crunch and immediately following the unprecedented recapitalisation of Europe's banks by governments across the continent, indeed of banks in many countries around the world.

Writing so close to epoch-changing events like these is fraught with danger. Who now agrees with those who declared as the Berlin Wall fell that we were witnessing the end of history or with the *Le Monde* writer who declared in the wake of 9/11 that "we are all Americans now"? With the benefit of a longer perspective, things can look quite different. Maybe the Chinese leader who explained that it was too early to assess the real impact of the French revolution was the wiser man.

Having entered those caveats, recent events do seem to offer powerful support to the notions that globalisation is a real phenomenon that leaves governments around the world with much less freedom of manoeuvre than they might once have thought they had, and that the solutions on which they have seized are much more similar than they are different. They lend powerful support also to the idea that in the digital age events can move at lightning speed, forcing governments to react much more quickly than would have been the case in even the recent past.

They seem to highlight as fallacy the thought that investment bankers were ever really "masters of the universe", to show that even central banks can be relatively powerless and to reveal, perhaps surprisingly, that governments, by contrast, can still move mountains – especially when they work together.

Finally, they throw a rather unflattering light on the role of the European Commission and the European Parliament, both rendered largely irrelevant by their lack of resources and their inability to act quickly. You can enjoy a lively debate about the relative importance of Gordon Brown, Nicolas Sarkozy or Angela Merkel in this moment of crisis, but few will seriously advance the claims of Jose Manuel Barroso or Hans-Gert Poettering. So much for the notion that it is in moments of crisis above all that the EU moves decisively towards "ever closer union".

Now as governments across Europe and around the world seek to shelter their people as best they can from the impact of recession or depression, it seems likely that many will reach for the same Keynesian tools of higher public spending, with higher public debt (with little regard paid to the European Commission's views on that subject).

All of which seems to point strongly in the direction of the role of government (and, by extension, lobbying) being much the same everywhere.

Yet if you look at not just at what politicians do, but also at what they say, it is clear that old ideological differences remain not far below the surface. Listen to Hank Paulson, the US Treasury Secretary, describe how what he was doing was necessary, but un-American, and contrast that with the glee with which Nicolas Sarkozy talks of the bankruptcy of the Anglo-American model of capitalism. Look at the enthusiasm with which the politicians of Europe pressed for a global summit on a new world order, but note how the *Wall Street Journal* chooses this moment to suggest that the (French) head of the IMF might be too distracted by other issues to take a leadership role.

From all of which I incline to the view that understanding government requires an understanding of difference and that even in today's world "all politics is local", as a former Speaker of the US House of Representatives famously put it.

So for the public affairs practitioner to be truly effective he or she must not only understand human nature (and especially what motivates politicians, officials and other stakeholders), but also have a profound understanding of institutional and cultural differences (or know a man or woman who does).

On the institutional level, for example, recent events remind us how very different are the political frameworks in the US and Europe. In the US the separation of powers between the executive and legislature required the Bush administration to secure the support of Congress for what it wanted to do, securing only a result only with the help of a tumbling stock market and the addition to the legislation of a raft of traditional pork barrel measures.

By contrast, the leaders of Europe's governments were able to take decisions with little or no need to woo their parliamentarians. This was so even in countries with coalition governments like Germany, where Angela Merkel took full advantage of the extensive powers of the Federal Chancellery.

It is that basic institutional contrast (over simplified, of course) that dictates major differences in the practice of public affairs on each side of the Atlantic, with US colleagues paying huge attention to coalition-building in Congress (and to grassroots and "grass tops" campaigning), while in Europe's capitals far more attention is focussed on the executive in general and the centre of government (10 Downing Street, the Elysee Palace, the Federal Chancellery) in particular. Perhaps nowhere is that more so than in Berlin, where the Chancellor's office maintains a shadow department for each Ministry and where the Head of the Federal Chancellery oversees all government decision-making.

Beyond such basic similarities between national capitals in Europe, there are also, of course, huge differences, which readily become apparent in the course of pan-European campaigns and from observation and discussion with colleagues.

Perhaps the most fundamental of these relate to the degree of federalism or centralisation in each country, with France at the centralised end of the spectrum, Belgium the most extreme federal case and Germany, with its powerful *lander*, the most important of all Europe's federal countries. Much depends too on the sector involved – a good example being health in Italy, where most of the decisions that really matter are taken at regional level.

Almost as fundamental are striking differences in the relative influence of national Parliaments, with France again offering one extreme (where significant parliamentary initiatives remain rare) and Denmark the opposite case (where, famously, governments receive their mandate on EU policy from the *Folketing*).

Across Europe public affairs practitioners agree that their work is about much more than direct lobbying of decision-makers and extends to mapping a wide range of stakeholders and devising appropriate means to engage in dialogue with them. Even so, there are wide variations in the perceived importance of different stakeholder groups.

Take the media – relevant in all countries, but more so in some than others. Arguably, for example, the traditional print and broadcast media have relatively little influence in Italy, since so much of it is owned or dominated by Silvio Berlusconi – with the result that some Italian bloggers have quite a high degree of influence.

It is a somewhat similar story in France, where, with the partial exception of *Le Monde*, the Paris-based print media have low circulations and not so much influence, a factor again in the relatively high importance of political bloggers in France. However, not to be under-estimated, ever since its foundation in 1915, is the influence of the satirical weekly, *Le Canard enchaine*, distinctly more important than its UK equivalent, *Private Eye*.

In the UK, traditional broadcast and print media retain huge influence, with well-sourced reports by the BBC economics correspondent, Robert

Peston, having the ability to move markets. British Prime Ministers and opposition leaders continue to go to considerable lengths to court newspapers like the *Daily Mail* and *The Sun* – and on occasion one may conclude that such newspapers have the ability to defeat even well-resourced lobbying campaigns. A quite well-known example would be the success of the *Mail's* campaign to block the opening of big new casinos in the UK, though that case also illustrates the often symbiotic relationship between newspapers and politicians since, in that example the *Mail* was encouraged to launch its campaign by the then Chancellor of the Exchequer, Gordon Brown.

Then look at the varying influence of NGOs, especially those representing consumer groups and environmental concerns. In some Mediterranean countries their role remains limited, as governments continue to listen more to traditional producer interests. At the opposite extreme are the Scandinavian countries, where these groups retain huge weight, no matter what the political colour of the government of the day. Similarly, the trade unions are still powerful in Sweden, France and Italy, but well past their peak in the UK. The significance of trade associations varies too, with German associations notably having a constitutional right to be heard in policy formulation.

Few public affairs practitioners would disagree that differences in institutional structures dictate, to a large extent, how and where their campaigns are conducted. There is probably less consensus about the degree to which cultural differences impact on the practice of public affairs, partly because practitioners are themselves often barely conscious of these differences, while nevertheless sub-consciously adjusting their ways of operating to reflect them.

Even to raise the subject is to risk accusations of racism, prejudice and stereotyping, but, it seems to me, that to ignore it completely runs an opposite risk – namely, that your public affairs campaigns will be less than optimally successful, as their insensitivity to national mores risks them being branded as insensitive and even alien to national interests.

At the most basic and obvious level there is language and it is clearly essential, where possible, to address decision-makers in their own language and also in the language appropriate to the interests represented – so fighting for the interests of, say, an SME in rural France, while deploying briefing papers written in American English doesn't make any kind of sense.

American and British English are quite different languages and an awareness of that can be important. Even the same word can mean different things, depending on the speaker. So, for example, a speaker from the US will happily use the word "aggressive" in a positive sense, as conveying energy, enthusiasm and determination. By contrast, a speaker from the UK would probably avoid the word as too confrontational.

While non-native English speakers in Europe may often disagree with the content of what an American colleague or competitor is saying, they can generally understand it. By contrast, Britons so regularly deploy understatement and humour that their Continental interlocutors are often baffled by what is meant. Too often this generates serious misunderstandings and on occasion, as a result, accusations about "perfidious Albion".

The way in which different nationalities use language can often reflect deeper cultural differences. So, for example, the Dutch can sometimes sound rude and blunt when all they are doing is reflecting the national desire to be straightforward and honest. In the Netherlands the opinions of all are valued and sought, without too much attention being paid to position in a hierarchy – hence the famous "polder model" where a consensus-based decision-making model, in which everyone has their say, is preferred. By contrast in a number of other European countries (including France, Germany and Italy) position in the hierarchy remains an important consideration.

Most European countries have some sense of what constitutes the ideal society, perhaps none more so than Sweden where the national consensus on fairness and equality, in particular (though also on the environment) runs very deep and is entertainingly described (or perhaps caricatured) in *Fishing in Utopia*, a thoughtful memoir published earlier this year by the British journalist, Andrew Brown. So convinced are most Swedes of the merits of their model that they sometimes seem the most convinced of all nations as they seek to export elements of it to their less fortunate neighbours.

One could easily write a whole book on the place of food and drink in public affairs and, an associated theme, of differences of attitude to working hours. At the risk of descending into cliché, one might suggest that, as so often, the Americans and French symbolise two very different approaches. Quite a few US lobbyists do like working breakfasts, do regard wine at lunchtime as the probable mark of an alcoholic and fret that a comfortable dinner with politicians might fall foul of the Foreign and Corrupt Practices Act. By contrast for quite a number of their French colleagues the *carnet d'adresses* retains great importance and convivial lunches and dinners remain important venues for significant discussions.

Though they are often very good at it, the French somehow even retain a certain haughty disdain for "lobbying", which some view as a kind of Anglo-Saxon perversion – Bertrand Delanoe, Mayor of Paris, famously declaring that London had beaten Paris to the 2012 Olympics not on merit, but because of "lobbying".

At a relatively trivial level, it is important also to know something of working hours' culture to avoid wasting time in doomed attempts to make contact "out of hours". For Spain, especially Madrid, much of the afternoon is still a no-go area, while in much of northern Europe many offices will be completely deserted after 5.30 p.m. It is a similar story when it comes to holidays, as Rome and Paris still close down for most of August, while it can be a the same story in Copenhagen and Stockholm in July.

Then there is religion. While, in their different ways, Catholic and Lutheran heritages combine with food, geography and climate to shape national cultures, the reality is that, in sharp contrast to the United States, the European public arena is increasingly a religion-free space – note, for example, how little impact the views of the Catholic Church had in thwarting the social reforms pursued by the government of Jose Luis Zapatero (Prime Minister of NATO ally, Spain, Senator McCain, not a Mexican drug runner). Look too at how in much of Europe, again notably France, private life and public service are seen as different domains, well illustrated by the relaxed French response to news of President Mitterrand's mistress and daughter and more recently to news of the pregnancy of the glamorous, unmarried Justice Minister, Rachida Dati ("My private life is complicated and I am keeping it off-limits to the media").

It is a matter of opinion, of course, but overall my feeling is that, while less important than institutional differences, cultural differences do have some impact on the practice of public affairs across Europe and that the best practitioners are those with the sensitivity to adapt accordingly.

Finally: just a few words about the institutions and culture of Brussels. Many other ECPA members are better-placed to offer more informed comment than I am, but it does seem to me that the European Union institutions have some interesting and special characteristics that do impact on EU public affairs practice.

Institutionally and (originally) linguistically, Brussels may seem a familiar place to the French, with its *Cabinets* in the Commission and its Rapporteurs in the Parliament, but, despite that superficial familiarity, it actually has some unique and remarkable features of its own.

Strikingly, it shares with North Korea the peculiarity of a legislative arm, the Council, which meets behind closed doors (despite Scandinavian attempts to promote transparency). Largely as a result, the most important common currency in the Brussels village is not the euro, but gossip and intelligence. Lobbyists need to know what the Council is doing and for this they turn, most frequently, to the permanent representations of the 27 national governments (the "permreps"). What has developed is a lively market place where the officials share vital information about behind closed door meetings, while, in return, the practitioners offer insight into the impact of EU proposals on their companies and clients.

Never is this more important than in the closing stages of debate on a Directive, when the three institutions (Council, Parliament and Commission) seek to forge agreement through a trialogue, a somehow ugly word that captures the involvement of all three in the process that ends with a new piece of European legislation.

Officially, of course, only the Council and the Parliament are legislators. In practice, especially, but not only, during the Presidency of a small country, the Commission plays a key role in floating ideas which may help the two other institutions to compromise and the Commission itself to secure safe passage for the Directive which it originally authored.

Public affairs practitioners in Brussels display their true worth as they demonstrate a clear understanding of this kind of process (and the Euro-culture on which it is based), especially when they can advise on how reality may differ from what the text book suggests – so that is not just about the special position of the Commission, but also, for example, about the fact that important conversations between the three institutions often begin long before they are openly acknowledged.

It is worth remembering also that all three are themselves lobbyists, with clear and distinct interests to advance. British MEPs, for example, are especially familiar with the sophisticated lobbying reach of the UK government, whose practice and style of lobbying is increasingly being copied by other governments.

In conclusion, it seems to me that the ECPA has been right from the outset in its dual approach – on the one hand, keeping practitioners up-to-date with developments in the working of the EU institutions, while on the other emphasising the importance of understanding national traditions. Those who have participated in ECPA's "sharing and learning" sessions will know that, more often than not, they seek to strike a balance between highlighting similarities in the experiences of practitioners across Europe and illuminating differences.

5. *Social Media – An Unmissable Opportunity for Public Affairs?*

Amber Price

Citizens increasingly question the undemocratic and unresponsive nature of the European institutions. This is a phenomenon we have seen developing in the media and during discussions over the "Treaty for Europe" (the Lisbon Treaty). In effect, the European institutions continue to suffer from a perceived communications deficit. Social Media appears to be one way that policy-makers are responding to these concerns, by engaging with a popular communications medium and attempting to bridge the gap, bringing citizens and policy-makers closer together.

Social Media is a relatively new phenomenon, and as such, a standardised definition is not commonly recognised. One challenge is that the online domain changes and adapts so rapidly that definitions fast go out of date. According to Wikipedia (a Social Medium in itself), the term Social Media refers to "activities that integrate technology, social interaction, and the construction of words, pictures, videos and audio". In essence they are online tools and platforms that people use to share information, opinions and experiences with each other. Social Media can take many different forms, including online forums, web logs (blogs), wikis, podcasts, pictures and video. Some examples of applications that employ Social Media are YouTube, My Space, Facebook and Second Life. So why would any of these have a role in the public affairs domain?

Some public affairs professionals are already taking tentative steps into this lesser known communications territory. This is happening in two distinct areas. The first is indirectly through the development and adoption of grassroots campaigns, working with consumer groups and the not-for-profit community, towards common campaigning goals. This is the activist approach and aims at government as one of a number of stakeholder groups. The second is more direct influence through, for example, online consultations and government hosted web chats, usually initiated by government. These are for the most part voluntary, but provide a means for public affairs practitioners to directly influence government stakeholders in the online domain.

Yet, the eternal question is should we respond in a more meaningful way? And, if so, how can we make use of this communications medium less *ad hoc* and thus more mainstream? A clear first step is to assess whether our key stakeholders – policy-makers – are truly using Social Media as a policy-making tool. Historically the European institutions have been slow to adopt modern communication technology and this is a key contributor to the perceived political communications deficit. In recent years, however, the European institutions have begun to re-focus their efforts to improve communications with their stakeholders. Key politicians and decision-makers have begun to adopt Internet communication tools (i.e. forms of Social Media) in an attempt to better communicate their message, and also to bring themselves closer to citizens and key stakeholders. We have also seen a call to action from Commissioner Wallström stating that it is time for the Commission "to embrace the Internet culture and online communications opportunities"[1]. This followed the release of an Action Plan to Improve Communicating Europe[2], a Communication outlining the European Commission's contribution to the reflection period on the Plan-D for democracy dialogue and debate and a White Paper on a European Communication Policy[3].

What does this mean in practise though? Although work is being done to assess how best to communicate with citizens, this work is not widely known. Aside from this general call to action, are the policy-makers we interact with on a regular basis actually adopting these methods as a core part of their toolbox? As ever, the answer is sometimes and in some circumstances. The use of Social Media has by no means been adopted consistently across the European institutions.

That said, we have seen the advent of internet consultations, online fora (sometimes labelled virtual meeting places), web chats and You Tube campaigns, all crafted by policy-makers. E-democracy, e-engagement and e-consultation have all become comfortable additions to the public affairs practitioner's vocabulary. For example, Commissioner Kuneva hosted a web chat on toy safety in 2007 which is a very good example of stakeholder engagement on a clear and very topical public policy issue.

1. European Commission (2007) *Communicating About Europe via the Internet: Engaging the Citizens*, SEC(2007) 1742; p. 3.
2. European Commission (2005) *Communication to the Commission: Action Plan to Improve Communicating Europe by the Commission*, SEC(2005) 985.
3. European Commission (2006) *White Paper on a European Communication Policy*, COM(2006) 35.

Yet use of the online domain seems to be fairly *ad hoc* and dependent on the policy-maker in question. There is a definite perception that it is the individual who decides on whether or not to, for example, commission a blog in their name (whether they themselves write it or have their staff do it). From a public affairs perspective too we have seen a tentative and perhaps half-hearted approach towards adopting Social Media in public affairs strategies, with the majority of examples coming from the NGO community. The tools are there (for example EurActiv's recently launched Blogactiv) but perhaps not the impetus.

In the broader PR arena we have seen the "to use or not to use?" question debated heavily when discussing the development and adoption of Social Media. There has been a recent shift in perception of public affairs from being considered one strand of PR alongside media relations, corporate communications and shareholder relations to it being considered a field in its own right. For the purposes of this debate, comparison to the other public relations disciplines is useful as we try to identify the role of Social Media for public affairs. For the most part in these other disciplines, it is widely accepted that the use of Social Media can work effectively, reaching a global audience, at a low cost, in real time and by anyone who has access to the Internet. Yet it is clear to see how this may cause more difficulties for public affairs practitioners.

The use of Social Media has fairly significant implications on the traditional relationship between policy-maker and public affairs practitioner. This is due to the role's strong emphasis on personal contact and face-to-face networking. Rather than bringing people closer together and breaking down barriers as in the other strands of public relations, Social Media causes more distance and therefore more communications barriers. This is why the function may struggle more with the distance of the Internet in relation to Social Media when compared to other communications functions.

There are links to the notion of trust where the face-to-face meeting and looking the contact in the eye has always been perceived as a critical part of relationship building. The concept of hierarchy is also important here. One of the biggest challenges is that online communications put the communicator on the same level as the subject because the sense of hierarchy is lacking. Identity is also often unclear; quite often a web host is actually behind the content, despite many pages publishing an "author". This could be a clear drawback for traditional and often hierarchical policy-makers.

Reciprocity is another notion that has traditionally been important in the communication between policy-maker and public affairs practitioner. According to Titley[4], the shift from an "elite/monologue" culture to "stakeholder/dialogue" culture is one of the biggest challenges for public affairs professionals. Despite the two-way communications channels of Social Media, rules of reciprocity are undefined and having a clear "ask" is not always easy. Still further, given the amount of information available, the fight to be "heard" online is a big money business with Google and others surviving very nicely from this niche market. This means that a public affairs message may not get through to the right person in order to influence the legislative process. It is likely that for these reasons we are seeing some reticence towards fully embracing the participative, mass communication of Social Media.

Unclear boundaries for the success or failure of a Social Media campaign are another reason that we remain on the periphery of mainstream use of Social Media. The perceived difficulty of reviewing success is also a barrier to wide use. It is likely that the addition of metrics for use of Social Media would encourage the integration of Social Media when developing public affairs strategies. This would then lead to these new tools becoming more widely used in practise, which is important because the benefits of use of Social Media do outweigh the perceived disadvantages.

Perhaps in fact this benchmarking should start at the level of the individual practitioner. Here is your call to action! By educating ourselves about the use of Social Media and by responding to developments in this field we can ensure we remain both in and ahead of the game. We must arm ourselves with all the tools needed to be able to maintain a competitive advantage and to best serve both corporate interest, public interest and the needs of policy-makers. Also by using these tools in practice, others will follow and use of Social Media in a public affairs campaign will become more mainstream.

4. Titley, S. (2003) "How Political and Social Change will Transform the EU Public Affairs Industry", *Journal of Public Affairs*, 3(1), pp. 83-89.

At an organisational level, we need to arm ourselves with metrics and benchmarks to ensure we strive for success and maximum efficiency. It is surely up to individual corporate affairs teams to monitor and agree metrics for these tools as they do for existing tools and strategies. Yet can any one company or group shift the landscape enough for Social Media to become mainstream? Perhaps not.

One way to address this is to open the debate at industry associations and think tanks to develop practical and tangible recommendations. This would be a clear step forward from the rather fragmented and inconsistent nature of the consultancy effort up to now. In their defence, it has been a sterling effort, but we must all push to broaden and develop the debate, on both sides of the table. Until the boundaries begin to be formed by one group or another, the use of Social Media in public affairs strategies risks remaining static.

It is hard to foresee a time when the use of Social Media would replace all other modes of communication, but it could easily be complementary to other modes of communication in a public affairs strategy. This is particularly true in the light of the ongoing transparency debate and moves towards increased scrutiny of practitioner and policy-maker alike. In effect, we have entered an age where traditional means of communicating in the public affairs sphere are changing fundamentally. It is how we step up to the challenge that will shape the nature of the relationship between practitioner and policy-maker and therefore the future of public affairs.

Part III. POLITICS AND PUBLIC AFFAIRS

1. *Of Rogues, Bishops and Golden Toads*
Tom Spencer

Governments, like fish, rot from the head. Over time the deadly mixture of ideology, money and power leads to a lazy hubris and a deadly belief in their own rhetoric. They come to despise any opposition, ignore bad news and rely on techniques of political manipulation rather than broad public support. A single external challenge can then destabilise the whole rotten structure. Mr Blair and President Bush are widely regarded as being punished by their electorates for the Iraq fiasco. In my view, Iraq is the trigger rather than the driver for the destruction of both their reputations. The Blair Government has used spin more relentlessly than any of its predecessors. It built a governing coalition, centralised power around a small group, politicised much of the civil service and then turned to deceit to fund its electoral needs. Cash for peerages is a story of rogues who took short cuts. George W. Bush presented himself in the 2000 election as a "Compassionate Conservative", squeaked into office on the votes of the Supreme Court rather than the electorate and then proceeded to construct a disciplined, centralised and dogmatic power structure. His addiction was not to spin, rather it was to control. Tom Delay's so-called "K Street Project" set out to restrict access to power to ensure that loyalists would be heard and rewarded. Had it succeeded it would have perverted the nature of public affairs in Washington. Over six years even the political genius of Karl Rove decayed into the constant repetition of tired stunts to "rally the base".

One of the wisest observers of the Washington public affairs scene confirms my instinct that the culture of corruption in Washington did have an impact on the elections. *"Back in January, only 18% of the public said that political corruption was a major issue for them. This led the GOP leadership in the House to conclude (erroneously) that if they waited long enough the scandals would fade from view. What they didn't realize was that public cynicism about politics and politicians was already dangerously high; the Abramoff scandal did in fact upset people, but they didn't consider it an 'issue' because they didn't feel empowered to do anything about it. Then came the Duke Cunningham bribery scandal, the resignation of Bob Ney and finally the Mark Foley incident. The cumulative effect – just in time for the election – cost the Republicans a lot of votes. When the exit polls were taken, something like 40% of the public said that 'political corruption' influenced their vote".* That 40% is more potent than a similar 40% who said they voted to express their concern about Iraq because it is spread more evenly across the electorate. Abramoff could credibly be dismissed as a corrupt rogue, but the smell of arrogance and corruption in the mismanagement of the occupation of Iraq – symbolised by Vice President Cheney's former company Halliburton – fed back into disillusion at home. Both Blair and Bush have recently been heavily criticised by their own top military. They stand accused of exposing their armies in ill-prepared, under-manned and under-equipped situations. "Dodgy Dossiers" and the shame of Abu Ghraib sink deep into the public consciousness.

How their successors in Democrat or Conservative administrations clean up this public affairs and governmental mess is a story for another day, but it is already apparent that the whirlwind of climate change is likely to be the next external challenge to political creativity. As always, effective global action in time depends on Washington not London. *American Theocracy: The Perils and Politics of Radical Religion, Oil and Borrowed Money in the 21ˢᵗ Century*, by Kevin Phillips (an advisor to Richard Nixon) underlines the role which petroleum money has played in American power from the beginning of the oil age. He spins off the elegant thought that this is typical of *"problems that all nations have to contend with as they grow older. The very sources of national success, whether in resources or industrial innovation, eventually reach their limits; what lasts is the structure of power and influence that inhibits reform".* This year has been full of good examples. One can sympathise with the crucifixion of Ford and General Motors until one remembers that it was motor industry lobbyists who ignited the SUV boom by lobbying for the deceit that such vehicles were "light trucks" not subject to motor car emission standards.

In my 15-year involvement with climate change as a political and public affairs issue I cannot remember a moment of such sea change in public attitudes. High oil prices with little prospect of long term relief seem to have succeeded where a hundred environmentalist documentaries have failed. They have changed the public and political sense of what is possible. In the 1960s R.A.B. Butler argued that politics was the art of the possible. Two generations later David Cameron feels comfortable bidding to become Prime Minister on the basis of green taxation that for the first time treats the public as adults in terms of the threat from climate change. Gordon Brown consequently re-positions himself around the Stern Report and suddenly all major political parties in the UK are aligned in favour of serious action. With any luck this sea change will spur political action in time to moderate the rise of sea levels that threaten to inundate Shanghai, Bangladesh, Florida and much of Manhattan. Is it too soon to take comfort from the increasing number of politicians of the Centre Right who are at last taking environmental issues seriously? David Cameron in the UK, John McCain in Arizona, Arnold Schwarzenegger in California and, after the Climate Change Conference in Nairobi, even President Barroso in Brussels. How will this interest interact with the increasing insistence of churchmen that environmental chaos is a moral as well as political and technical issue?

Taxing aviation fuel is a good case in point. We have known for many years that airlines are major perpetrators of global warming. I remember discussions with both British Airways and KLM in the early 1990s, which always ended in evasion and guilty silence. Cheap air flights have helped build a sense of Europe, and their curtailment might endanger that tenuous sense of European unity that sets in just before the hangover. The growth in flights remains as strong as predicted, but its impact on the climate becomes more obvious as other sources are contained or reduced and as we learn more about its damage to the atmosphere. I recently had cause to ponder my attitude to cheap air flight. I was in California when the great "liquids can blow you out of the sky" story broke. For once it seemed to me that it was the British who were over-reacting, while the American public, perhaps for the first time, refused to be panicked by the fear machine of the Bush Administration. Maybe, I mused, there is a Gaia-like countervailing force at work. The more we yearn for cheap air flight, the more we are rewarded with Islamic fundamentalists and deep vein thrombosis. Richard Chartres, the excellent Bishop of London, whose presence has for some years been my main anchor in the Church of England, had stolen the summer headlines a few weeks before with his meditation on environmental sins and his conclusion that serious Christians should no longer take polluting long-distance holidays. Yet here I was in an American desert, soaking up the sunshine while writing panegyrics in praise of Al Gore's movie on climate change, *An Inconvenient Truth*.

We may have to abandon the old reference to "shifting the deck chairs on the Titanic", if the Greenland ice cap melts and icebergs in the North Atlantic become a thing of the past. The sheer scale of mankind's impertinence was borne out to me while standing in a field of soya beans carved out of the Amazon rainforest near Santarem. From the air the area looks like beautifully planted English parkland, with copses flanking expanses of open farmland, graced by carefully preserved individual trees. On the ground the truth is altogether more serious. The "copses" are signs of the developers' determination to avoid the regulation that at least 20% of the jungle must be left standing. The single trees are Brazil Nut trees. However stately they look in their splendid isolation, every one of them is doomed. The Brazil Nut is protected under Brazilian law, but it is a protection that is meaningless once the forest has been stripped away. The tree is a forest species. It is fertilised by a single type of bee. The bee depends on a particular orchid which grows within height range of the Brazil Nuts. Once the surrounding trees and their orchids are removed, the bee no longer fertilises the flowers of the Brazil Nut and the tree becomes infertile. However it is not destined to suffer this infertility for long, as, stripped of its surrounding forest, it is inevitably killed by direct sun and wind. These micro-tragedies, caused in equal part by Europe's hunger for soya to feed its meat eating frenzy and Brazil's equation of the forest with under-development, threaten much greater tragedies. Sharing this sorry sight with me was another Bishop, James Jones, the Anglican Bishop of Liverpool who was being interviewed by the BBC. The interviewer pointed out that much of Liverpool's traditional wealth had been based on the slave trade. By extension they were keen to know James's views on the ethics of soya exports from Cargill's new terminal at Santarem directly into Liverpool. Within days of the publicity given to this issue, the soya companies had promised a moratorium on further soya-led forest destruction. Suddenly good public affairs had made the impossible possible.

I was in Brazil for the sixth meeting of the Religion, Science and the Environment Symposium led by the remarkable "green" Patriarch of Constantinople, the head of the Orthodox Church. In the extraordinary surroundings of the Manaus Opera House, relic of the 19th Century rubber boom, His All Holiness was declared by the Governor of Manaus State to be the Patriarch of the Rainforest. In an extraordinary shift for the head of a major Christian Church, the Patriarch has encouraged all Christians to recognise and value indigenous peoples and their religious experience. It is not surprising that third generation environmentalism is increasingly drawing on religious and scientific insight.

The Symposium's time in Manaus revealed yet darker secrets. The uninitiated might reasonably believe that the Amazon rainforest exists because there is a lot of rain. As a result of recent scientific work in Amazonia, we now know that the rain falls because of the forest. Without the forest releasing its volatile organic compounds to seed the rising water vapour that it emits daily, the area risks the unthinkable fate of becoming a desert. Drought has already struck parts of the North East of Brazil as the damaged "forest pump" fails to suck in sufficient warm air from the southern part of the North Atlantic. This leaves the sea temperatures in the birthing grounds of Caribbean hurricanes dangerously high. For years the sophisticated Brazilian Foreign Office has pumped out elegant diatribes about Brazil's right to follow Europe in clearing its domestic forests. Now those same diplomats may like to try explaining to the Caribbean, Mexico and the USA the logic of their forest clearance projects as made manifest in Hurricane Katrina. More immediately useful for the public affairs of the possible is the growing recognition that destruction of the Amazon forest cover is reducing rainfall in the food baskets of southern Brazil and the rich pampas of Argentina. There is now an impeccable case, rooted in Brazilian self-interest, for calling a halt to soya-led rainforest destruction. Last year Sao Paulo's eighteen million people came within ten days of running out of drinking water. While this would have made an interesting case study for the Institute for Environmental Security, it would certainly have added a security dimension that would have enriched Brazil's environmental consciousness!

Those of you who have followed my argument thus far may be anxious to know where the golden toad comes in. For the full story I refer you to an excellent book, The Weather Makers, by Tim Flannery. Its sub-title is, "The History and Future Impact of Climate Change". It is a compendium of stories elegantly told to illustrate our arrogance and carelessness. For me, its most emotive story is set in the Monteverde Cloud Forest in Costa Rica. The golden toad *(Bufo periglenes)* was only discovered in 1966. It spent most of its life underground in burrows, emerging above ground during the wet season in April and May. The details of toad mating are not a fit matter for public affairs practitioners, but suffice it to say that the males used every trick in the book to gain access to the female in what is euphemistically described as a "toad ball". Think lobbyists pursuing a European Parliament Rapporteur. In 1987 the clouds failed to deliver sufficient moisture to the forest pools near the top of the mountain. The eggs were desiccated and by the following May researchers could locate only a single male, the last of his species. As the climate warms species such as the toad are either driven further up the mountain or they die. The world's politicians need to recognise that they do not have much head room left.

Now that we begin to understand what drives it, it is not the difficulty of countering climate change which is so depressing. Rather it is the agonising slowness with which our species sorts out its political responses and unpicks the public affairs knots so carefully woven by previous politicians and special interests. We will never see the golden toad again, but in 2007 we can at least contemplate the possibility that *Homo sapiens sapiens* may just get its act together in time… even if that means that I have to abandon an outdated worship of sunshine.

Originally written as an ECPA Briefing, November 2006.

2. *A Novel Look at Lobbyists*

Conor McGrath

There have always been occasional works of fiction (novels, movies, TV shows, songs, and so on) which have dealt with political issues or institutions, but the last decade has seen a much more concerted trend in this direction. Clearly, the most successful and long-lasting marriage between fiction and politics has been *The West Wing*, but there have been many others – movies like *The American President, Dave, Wag the Dog*, television programmes such as *Yes, Minister, The Thick of It, K Street*[1], *Commander in Chief*, novels like *Primary Colors*, the *House of Cards* series by Michael Dobbs, Carl Hiaasen's Florida satires, and Robert Harris' *The Ghost*.

There is, in addition, a substantial body of academic work by now on the fictional portrayal of political actors and institutions, ranging from highly theoretical discussion of how particular ideologies appear in classic literature to debate over the realism of *The West Wing*. While fiction aims to entertain, the creators of fictional work are doubtless not unaware that they also inform and educate. Public views about politics are formed – at least in part – through the ways in which politics is represented in fiction. While we have no scholarly research into the role which fictionalised accounts of politics play in contributing to any public dissatisfaction with or mistrust of lobbyists, we could intuitively expect that there is some connection between what the average citizen watches or reads in popular culture and what he or she thinks about politics. This essay offers an overview of how lobbyists are presented in modern literature, and suggests that lobbyists will find little of comfort in their fictional counterparts.

Unhappily, most recent novels which feature lobbyists will not be inspirational reads from the perspective of practitioners. It is true that some provide quite full portrayals of both lobbying and lobbyists, but these are very much the exceptions to the rule – and even here, they tend merely to provide full accounts of the sexual and/or financial and/or political greed and lust of lobbyists. Most novels which have lobbyists as characters show them as relentlessly corrupt, unethical and predatory.

---

1. For a detailed discussion of this 2003 groundbreaking (though unsuccessful commercially) drama series set in a Washington lobbying firm, see McGrath, C. (2008) "*K Street*: 'Raping HBO' or 'What HBO Is All About'?", in Leverette, M., Ott, B. and Buckley-Ott, C. (eds.) *It's Not TV: Watching HBO in the Post-Television Era*, New York: Routledge; pp. 171-89.

Lobbyists are rarely treated in fiction with much subtlety, while gross characterisations of their personalities and misrepresentation of the role of lobbying are commonplace.

One satirical Irish novel opens with an aristocratic landowner telling Mick Flannery (the local MEP) that he wants Flannery to obtain EU funding to support a foxhunt: "'Look here, Michael old *chap*, it works something like this. You apply to the *blokes* in the European Commission for a Wildlife Grant to support the hunt, and that's all there is to it. As simple as falling off a log! All it needs is a spot of – what do you call it?' There was a longish pause during which his face contorted with the effort of finding the right word. Then, with a note of triumph in his voice, he continued, '*Lobbying*, that's the blasted word I wanted. Then the Brussels chappies say 'right ho' or 'tout bien' or whatever it is they say when everything is OK and above board. After that they start shoveling the money our way, *and Bob's your uncle!*'"[2]. Not a view that Brussels-based practitioners will want their bosses or clients to subscribe to!

Perhaps the best American satirist, Christopher Buckley, turned his gaze towards lobbying in a 1994 novel, *Thank You For Smoking*, which was later turned into a movie. In this novel, Nick Naylor is the lobbyist and chief spokesman of the Academy of Tobacco Studies – the trade association representing major cigarette companies. Naylor lunches regularly with two friends who are lobbyists for other products frowned upon by the liberal consensus: Bobby Jay Bliss, a pro-gun advocate (he works for "SAFETY, the Society for the Advancement of Firearms and Effective Training of Youth, formerly NRBAC, the National Right to Bear Arms Committee"[3]), and Polly Bailey, the chief spokesperson for the Moderation Council, "formerly the National Association for Alcoholic Beverages, [which] represented the nation's distilled spirits, wine and beer industries"[4]. The three lobbyists refer to themselves as the Mod Squad (or 'Merchants of Death'), due to the nature of the products they represent.

During an appearance on *Larry King Live*, Naylor receives a phoned-in death threat, live on air, and is soon afterwards kidnapped. His captors attempt to assassinate Nick by covering his body in nicotine patches, so that he receives a near-fatal dose. He escapes and his life is saved in hospital.

2. Binchy, D. (1992) *The Last Resort*, London: Century; p. 1.
3. Buckley, C. (1994) *Thank You For Smoking*, New York: Random House; p. 18.
4. Buckley, C. (1994) *Thank You For Smoking*, New York: Random House; p. 20.

During a breakfast television interview from his hospital room, Nick manages to use his experience to generate good publicity for the tobacco industry – first by insisting that, had he not been a smoker, his body could not have withstood the massive nicotine dose delivered by the patches, and secondly by suggesting that the industry was entirely reasonable and freedom-loving: "'Well, Katie, you can't spell tolerance without the *t* in *tobacco*.... This is a big country, and there's plenty of room in it for smoking *and* nonsmoking areas'"[5].

After a dinner with his colleague, Jeannette Dantine, Nick ends up in bed with her, during which she puts on latex gloves, saying that she thinks they are sexy, and gives him a packet of condoms to open. The following morning, Jeannette is gone before Nick wakens, and she has removed all the used condoms and empty boxes. Naylor returns to work to deal with a legislative challenge – Senator Finisterre of Vermont introduced a Bill which would oblige tobacco companies to put a skull and crossbones on the packets of their products, as a health warning for those immigrants unable to read English. During a debate with Finisterre, Nick rejects the need for any additional warnings on tobacco packets and suggests instead that the largest single deadly disease in America is not cancer caused by smoking, but rather cholesterol – "'I'm sure that the tobacco industry would consent to having these labels put on *our* products, if he [Finisterre] will acknowledge the *tragic* role that *his* product is playing, by putting the same warning labels on these deadly chunks of solid, low-density lipoprotein that go by the name of Vermont cheddar cheese'"[6].

Nick is arrested by the FBI for staging his own kidnap and assault in order to generate publicity. It transpires that the FBI have physical evidence against Nick, in the form of boxes of nicotine patches with his fingerprints on them which have been found in a rented cabin. He realises that he has somehow been set up by Jeannette, who transferred his fingerprints from the condom wrappers to the incriminating boxes of nicotine patches. Nick decides to plead guilty to the FBI charges; he reasons that his story would not be believed, that he couldn't afford the legal fees needed to mount a defence, and that he is any event guilty of, "'Crimes against humanity. Maybe it's just a mid-life crisis. I don't know. I'm tired of lying for a living'"[7]. The novel ends with Nick Naylor making another appearance on

---

5. Buckley, C. (1994) *Thank You For Smoking*, New York: Random House; p. 116.
6. Buckley, C. (1994) *Thank You For Smoking*, New York: Random House; p. 198.
7. Buckley, C. (1994) *Thank You For Smoking*, New York: Random House; p. 261.

Larry King Live about three years later. He has just been released from a minimum security prison where he served two and a half years for staging his own abduction. He has written a book exposing the tobacco industry and is now working for an anti-smoking lobby called Clean Lungs 2000. Nick's book is subtitled *Jujitsuing the Neo-Puritans*, which metaphor explains how he used to operate as a lobbyist: "'Well, as you know, jujitsu is the Japanese art of self-defense in which you use your opponent's weight and strength against him. That was really all I ever had to do. Though I certainly don't advocate smoking, there are some very sanctimonious people lined up on the nonsmoking side. So it was just a matter of giving them a little shove and putting my foot behind them'"[8].

Christopher Buckley is a satirist and as such he paints vivid pictures in broad strokes; satire deals in caricature rather than portraiture. That said, though, elements of Nick Naylor's personality and work life will be familiar to professional lobbyists. To take just one small but telling example – just as the members of the Mod Squad work for groups whose titles disguise their true interests, in the real world lobbying organisations often go to some lengths to devise a title which frames themselves and their issues in the best possible light. A report by the Washington-based Advocacy Institute noted some examples, including: the group representing pesticide manufacturers changed its name from the National Agricultural Chemicals Association to the more positive-sounding American Crop Protection Association; Citizens for Sensible Control of Acid Rain, which was established by energy utility companies in an effort to defeat proposals to curb acid rain; and the Alliance for Energy Security, which was really a creation of the Natural Gas Suppliers Association in its campaign to lobby for deregulation of the industry[9]. Buckley's eye for this sort of detail – based in reality, and stretched up to but not beyond the limits of credulity – is what makes his portrayal of lobbyists so engaging. Unlike most novelists, he presents lobbyists with a human face.

Many of the lobbyists encountered in works of fiction have a legal background and training. One character in a John Grisham novel is a lawyer, pondering on the motivation of colleagues working in his large firm: "the litigators were still the most revered of all God's lawyers, at least within the firm... Tax law was horribly complex, but its practitioners were greatly

---

8. Buckley, C. (1994) *Thank You For Smoking*, New York: Random House; p. 271.
9. Advocacy Institute (1995) *By Hook or by Crook: Stealth Lobbying – Tactics and Counterstrategies*, Washington, DC: Advocacy Institute.

admired. Governmental relations (lobbying) was repulsive but paid so well that every D.C. firm had entire wings of lawyers greasing the skids"[10]. Other fictional lobbyists are similarly attracted by money – one had played college football and was intending to become a professional American footballer until being injured in one game: "Steve had decided at that moment that there had to be an easier way than a football career to acquire the wealth and status he had always longed for.... when he'd learned about the influential, freewheeling, lucrative life of legislative lobbyists, he'd known that was the career he'd been born for"[11].

One of the more unusual political novels is *The Washington Fringe Benefit*, written by Elizabeth Ray, who actually worked as a secretary-receptionist in Washington for lobbyists and politicians. In 1976, she gave an interview to the *Washington Post* in which she described having had a series of sexual affairs with her employers, their clients and their colleagues. Her novel is a very thinly-veiled account of her time on Capitol Hill. In it, she describes an oil lobbyist, Elan Bright, for whom she worked: "Lobbyist Bright was fun-loving and God-fearing at the same time, and when he said, 'See you in church,' he meant it, even if we had been into the most unholy mischief the night before. His enviable reputation for persuasion almost equalled his fame as the employer of the most gorgeous girls on Capitol Hill"[12]. Without two weeks of employing her, Elan Bright and Elizabeth Ray (the lead character in the novel has the same name as the author) had sex together. Over the next few months, she was offered as a sexual partner to Elan Bright's contacts; on one occasion to a key Senator the night before a Senate vote on a piece of legislation which Bright was lobbying for. Eventually, Elizabeth Ray moved from Bright's office to work for Congressman Billie Bob Blank – "I could tell from our first meetings that he was interested in me, and I was pleased when he actually invited me to join his staff. Even my boss couldn't refuse the request of a Congressman from a major oil-producing state"[13].

By way of contrast, some works of fiction do give lobbyists romantic rather than sexually predatory roles. In *License To Love*, Steve Saraceni is a successful lobbyist in Pennsylvania who learns that his girlfriend, Michelle Carey (aide to a state senator) is pregnant. He is clearly a confident and

10. Grisham, J. (1998) *The Street Lawyer*, New York: Doubleday; p. 49.
11. Boswell, B. (1992) *License To Love*, New York: Silhouette Desire; p. 10.
12. Ray, E.L. (1976) *The Washington Fringe Benefit*, New York: Dell; p. 49.
13. Ray, E.L. (1976) *The Washington Fringe Benefit*, New York: Dell; p. 77.

personable character: "The image he projected appealed to both men and women alike. Approachable, eminently likable, earnest and honest. Lobbyists – and he was a lobbyist consultant representing a number of clients – were sometimes viewed as aggressive, slick and cool, but Steve Saraceni never came across that way. He had never met anyone he couldn't eventually charm into liking him"[14].

Fictional lobbyists appear to spend a great deal of time on entertaining and socialising. They are often mentioned in the context of fine dining. In one novel, a woman (from an organisation which monitors the activities of multinational pharmaceutical companies) discusses how these firms influence decisions made by the World Health Organisation: "'Go to any WHO assembly – what do you see?' she asked rhetorically, handing him a bunch of pamphlets. 'Lobbyists. PR people from the big pharmas. Dozens of them. From one big pharma, maybe three or four. "Come to lunch. Come to our weekend get-together. Have you read this wonderful paper by Professor So-and-So?" And the Third World is not sophisticated. They have no money, they are not experienced. With diplomatic language and manoeuvring, the lobbyists can get behind them easy'"[15]. The lobbyist-as-romantic lead, Steve Saraceni, mused aloud about his entertaining of politicians: "Lobbyists go to fund-raisers, parties, luncheons, and dinners on behalf of charities, cultural groups, political action committees and campaigns. You name it and we're there, wherever the state legislators are. The name of the game is access. Even the appearance of access is a large part of the exercise"[16].

A common feature of many works of fiction is that if lobbyists are only mentioned infrequently or in passing, it will almost always be in a derogatory fashion and will often relate to some corruption or unethical practice. So, for instance, in a prescient novel based around the US Electoral College, one character is described as "the child of a well-to-do Baton Rouge lawyer-lobbyist who had spent his life plying the legislators of Louisiana with whiskey and women"[17]. Similarly, one novel features a state governor with a "background as a lobbyist who dispensed girls like party favors"[18]. In another novel, after a Texas businessman is warned by a judge

---

14. Boswell, B. (1992) *License To Love*, New York: Silhouette Desire; p. 8.
15. le Carre, J. (2001) *The Constant Gardener*, London: Coronet; pp. 357-8.
16. Boswell, B. (1992) *License To Love*, New York: Silhouette Desire; pp. 49-50.
17. Greenfield, J. (1996) *The People's Choice*, New York: Plume; p. 18.
18. Patterson, R.N. (2008) *The Race*, Basingstoke: Macmillan; p. 258.

that "bribery of a public official is a felony", he simply smiles and replies that, "At the capitol in Austin we call it lobbying"[19].

In *Me* by Garrison Keillor, we are given a satirical account of the life of a former professional wrestler who is elected Governor of Minnesota. One of the reasons for this populist's decision to enter politics is his growing awareness of how politicians and lobbyists lead different life to those of the average American: "The votes of truck drivers count as much as those of people who read *The New York Times*. Politicians forget that. They think that getting elected makes them wise and elegant indeed. They sit in their royal chambers, wearing their French cuffs, and are addressed as My Distinguished Colleague and My Learned Friend and go off to a thirty-five-dollar lunch of linguini and shrimp and sun-dried tomatoes with some lobbyists in blue pinstripe suits who treat their every opinion as a precious pearl"[20].

Do some of these portrayals seem true to life? Are lobbyists in Brussels or London or Prague providing women to their clients? Are many primarily motivated by money? Are legislators as susceptible to flattery, bribery or fine cuisine in reality as they are in fiction? Fictional lobbyists are too often shown as sleazy, amoral and self-interested – in fact as parasites on the body politic. This highly subjective perspective is both caused by common (however vague or ill-informed) prejudices and in turn itself helps to perpetuate such prejudices. Moreover, popular culture signally fails to show a true reflection of the work on which professional lobbyists are engaged. These stilted stereotypes not only mislead the viewing and reading public, but contribute towards the fact that real political lobbyists are held in such low esteem by the general population.

Lobbyists present too easy a target for writers wanting to include in their political fiction a cardboard-cutout despoiler of democracy. Unfortunately, this view does then become adopted by consumers of popular culture. Lobbyists will find it difficult to enhance their public standing or reputation – and the electorate will continue to hold gross biases about a key and legitimate element of the political process – until novelists and screenplay writers begin to present more realistic and rounded lobbyists in their literary works.

19. Gimenez, M. (2008) *The Perk*, London: Sphere; p. 259.
20. Keillor, G. (1999) *Me*, London: Faber and Faber; p. 9.

To conclude on a more hopeful note, however, there are things which lobbyists can do to at least partially address this situation. Individuals – and particularly the leadership of associations which represent lobbyists – should make more strenuous efforts to educate the public about the legitimate role of lobbying in a democracy and the positive effects of lobbyists in representing interests. Through such work, the grosser mischaracterisations of lobbyists in fiction will ring false to a greater number of readers. In addition, lobbyists ought to proactively seek out opportunities to talk to novelists (and to those who write screenplays for films and TV dramas). Identify novelists whose work deals with political themes, and invite them to address meetings of lobbyists. Lobbyists could offer to speak to writers' groups. Look at the author's note which is increasingly common at the end of novels – see which political organisations have been consulted by novelists in researching their fiction, and be open to such approaches from writers in the future. The world of lobbying and public affairs is full of potential for fiction writers – real and substantial issues of public policy, conflict and compromise, human interest, drama and comedy. There are ways in which lobbying can be portrayed in a compelling yet true fashion – provided that lobbyists and novelists begin to talk to each other.

3. *The Public Affairs of Sunshine*
Tom Spencer

A year in which one half of Europe is roasted, while the other half drowns, looks set to see the whole continent adopting the British habit of talking endlessly about the weather. The political weather for the European Union seems to be benefiting from a shift in the intellectual jet stream. For the first time since the French and Dutch votes on the Constitution, believers in the European cause can feel sunlight on their faces. The June Summit that produced the draft Reform Treaty, went more smoothly than might have been expected. The combination of a successful German Presidency, a new French President and a British Prime Minister prepared to ignore demands for a referendum lifts the gloom that has pervaded European circles. There is every prospect of an end to the deadlock that was euphemistically described as "a pause for reflection". Eurosceptics will bemoan the resilience of the Union, while Europhiles will regret the loss of significant totems from the draft Constitution. However politicians, as opposed to public intellectuals, should welcome the outcome. They should also read Michael Ignatieff's op-ed piece in the *New York Times* on 5th August. As the ultimate public intellectual, who has chosen to leave his ivory tower in Harvard and launch into the choppy waters of Canadian politics, Ignatieff's musings should command respect:

> *"The philosopher Isaiah Berlin once said that the trouble with academics and commentators is that they care more about whether ideas are interesting than whether they are true. Politicians live by ideas just as much as professional thinkers do, but they can't afford the luxury of entertaining ideas that are merely interesting. They have to work with the small number of ideas that happen to be true and the even smaller number that happen to be applicable to real life. In academic life, false ideas are merely false and useless ones can be fun to play with. In political life, false ideas can ruin the lives of millions and useless ones can waste precious resources. An intellectual's responsibility for his ideas is to follow their consequences wherever they may lead. A politician's responsibility is to master those consequences and prevent them from doing harm... I've learned that good judgment in politics looks different from good judgment in intellectual life. Among intellectuals, judgment is about generalizing and interpreting particular facts as instances of some big idea. In politics, everything is what it is and not another thing. Specifics matter more than generalities. Theory gets in*

the way.... The attribute that underpins good judgment in politicians is a sense of reality. 'What is called wisdom in statesmen,' Berlin wrote, referring to figures like Roosevelt and Churchill, 'is understanding rather than knowledge – some kind of acquaintance with relevant facts of such a kind that it enables those who have it to tell what fits with what; what can be done in given circumstances and what cannot, what means will work in what situations and how far, without necessarily being able to explain how they know this or even what they know.' Politicians cannot afford to cocoon themselves in the inner world of their own imaginings. They must not confuse the world as it is with the world as they wish it to be. They must see Iraq – or anywhere else – as it is."

Both sides of the debate about Europe ignored the necessity to "see Europe as it is". Both were cocooned in their own frames of reference. In truth the European Union is neither an evil Teutonic plot nor a benign, carbon copy of the institutions of the Federal Republic of Germany. It is what it has always been, a *sui generis* response by the peoples of Europe to the challenge of peace in their continent and now to the defence of Europe's interests in the world. I feel a rare apology is appropriate. The Presidencies of large countries are normally a disappointment. On this occasion Angela Merkel delivered success on the three areas that matter most for this generation of Europeans – climate change, foreign policy and an updating of Europe's self image. Europe will now play a full role in the "great game" of squaring energy security, environmental stability and the attendant foreign policy challenges of a multi-polar world.

"Let sunshine win the day", cried David Cameron in his peroration at the Conservative Party Conference in October 2006. He flooded the conference platform with sunshine and blue skies. His advisors had rightly identified the lesson from American politics about the importance of optimism. Parties out of government need to hold out sunlit uplands, shining cities on the hill, if they are to overturn incumbents. Ten months later David Cameron has discovered that in the words of Longfellow: "Into each life some rain must fall". The commentariat that gave David Cameron a prolonged honeymoon now turn on him. Their central charge seems to be that he is all public relations and has no strategic vision. Even by the standards of media tittle-tattle, this is a thoroughly unjust accusation. David Cameron is the first Leader of the Conservative Party since Margaret Thatcher to have both a clear strategy for regaining power and the nerve to see it through. To win he needs to restore the credibility of the Conservative

Party and to win back the votes of the professional classes, women and young voters. He needs to have change on his side, even if this means temporarily discomforting the Party's right wing. Of necessity, this means using the tactical tools of public relations to shake up the congealed perceptions of ten years of right wing and Eurosceptic nastiness.

It says much for the image problem that public relations has as a profession in the UK when the very mention of it can be used as an insult. There ought to be a difference between "public relations" and "spin". For the ten years of Blair's Britain, spin meant endlessly re-packaging old announcements and an approach to the truth that should have shamed even Alastair Campbell. What could be more typical of Blair's "low dishonest decade" than that Campbell should feel it necessary to "edit" his diaries, *The Blair Years*, to avoid embarrassing the Labour Party? Gordon Brown has spun his way to a good start as Prime Minister by denouncing spin. He chooses to distance himself from Blair by puritanical rebuttal of the Labour Government's policies on gambling, licensing hours and the re-classification of cannabis. With Presbyterian certainty and statistical wizardry, he flourishes the science of skunk and dispatches the joys of social liberalism. He should be careful. Cavaliers are more in tune with modern Britain than Roundheads. There is a looming backlash against the loss of civil liberties during the last ten years. Brown will only make this stronger by his insistence on intrusive DNA identity cards and an assertive state that insists on using traffic data and CCTV cameras to track the movement of every citizen. Longer periods of internment without trial, and similar products of the politics of fear, fit too comfortably into the public's accumulated perceptions of Gordon Brown. He will not risk an early election and will be looking less fresh by the summer of 2009. The sunlight that temporarily surrounds him feels more like a golden sunset than a new dawn.

The ability of the Arctic ice to reflect the sun's rays back into space is a key part of the mechanism that inhibits global warming. The importance of the Arctic is only slowly penetrating the public consciousness. The concept of starving polar bears, separated from their prey by melting polar ice, has made it into the public discourse. The much greater dangers of methane release from melting tundra and the increased tendency for the land-based Greenland Glacier to both melt and slide into the Atlantic is taking longer to ring alarm bells. It is typical of the rearguard action being fought by the fossil fuel industries that they seek to cloud the picture by making much of those bits of Greenland which are getting colder, while ignoring the continuing dramatic loss of snow and ice cover. Scientific complexity will always offer opportunities for unscrupulous public affairs. The Arctic should properly be seen as the repository of much of the damage which industrial civilisation has inflicted on the planet. High latitudes are warming faster than the Equator and toxic chemicals build up most intensely in the Arctic food chain.

How appropriate therefore that the Arctic may well prove to be our nemesis. The retreat of the sea ice holds out the prospect for a great new bonanza of the very fossil fuels that are destabilising our environment. Rather than drawing the obvious conclusion that it would be unwise to extract this Faustian gold, the Arctic nations are now engaged in an unseemly scramble to plant their national flags. A longer term view would be to treat the Arctic in the same way that we have agreed to treat Antarctica by forbidding mineral exploitation. One might have thought that the International Polar Year 2007/2008 would be a good time to start. Full marks therefore for His All Holiness the Ecumenical Patriarch of Constantinople, who is taking this year's Religion, Science and Environment Symposium to the far North under the title "The Arctic: Mirror of Life". He rejected substantial financial support from the Norwegian Government when they insisted that the Symposium should celebrate the new potential for Statoil to deploy their drilling technology in Arctic regions. Instead His All Holiness is taking a group of 17 leaders of the world's faiths to the Icefjord on the West coast of Greenland, where many icebergs calve, to "Pray for the Planet".

Such issues are not merely of scientific and religious interest. Following a Spanish initiative, the Organisation for Security and Co-operation in Europe (OSCE) is giving serious thought to adding Environment and Security to its mandate and is encouraging its 54 member governments from Vancouver to Vladivostok, to develop their own Environment and Security programmes. Despite the fact that the Arctic is an OSCE lake, the complex of trade, transport and security issues make it too difficult a topic for them to tackle, with the Russians, Canadians and Americans all limiting themselves to comforting platitudes at frozen latitudes. Conflict, verging on war, over such resources is no longer the stuff only of dystopian nightmares.

The rhetoric of governments about the dangers of climate change has shifted recently in a positive direction, but there remain huge doubts about their real ability to make a difference. While the image of carbon trading has taken a battering from its association with dicey hedge funds and a fringe of bogus operators in the Voluntary Emissions Trading Market, nobody seriously doubts that it will be part of the solution. However there remains a major role for regulatory approaches. The Montreal Protocol is without any doubt the most climate-friendly treaty ever enacted, even if that was not its primary intent. The twentieth anniversary of the Protocol falls in September 2007 and a diverse group of nations want to celebrate it by agreeing a much faster rate for phasing out the remaining HCFCs. The silo mentality of government departments threatens however to kick this promising opportunity into the long grass by referring it to a study group. The strangely fickle nature of the political process seems doomed to concentrate on the small and difficult, while wilfully avoiding some obvious low hanging fruit.

Those of us who work in public affairs occasionally forget just how much influence we may have. I was recently asked by *Public Affairs News* to review Daniel Guéguen's new book, *European Lobbying*. It is beautifully laid out, wonderfully idiosyncratic, and in some areas, just plain wrong. Daniel draws heavily on his own experience in European Trade Associations in a way which, in my view, underplays the role of corporate lobbying and gives a rather old fashioned feel to his text. However he does give an interesting case study of the European Photovoltaic Industry Association (EPIA), which I have every reason to believe is accurate. One consequence of its success is that every politician in Europe who hears mention of solar power, thinks immediately of photovoltaic cells. Unfortunately, in the ruthless competition between renewables, that is an inevitable subset of the wider rivalry between renewables and fossil fuels, such carefully engineered perceptions have squeezed out the potentially much more important generator of power known as "Concentrated Solar Power" (CSP). CSP is proven technology involving using mirrors to concentrate the sun's rays and, in a variety of ways, to heat water to produce steam which drives a turbine. Large scale operations have existed in the Mojave Desert for 20 years and the Spanish have built a series of plants developing Californian technology. Why therefore does it not feature on most lists of exciting, upscaleable renewables?

The answer seems to lie almost entirely in the realm of public affairs. There is a nomenclature problem. Is it to be known as Concentrated Solar Power or Solar Thermal Power? If the latter, how is it to be distinguished from small scale projects aimed at heating domestic bath water. Then there is the absence of an effective trade association with any focus on Brussels. CSP works best in deserts of the kind found in North Africa and the South West States of the USA. Governments in gloomy Northern Europe tend not to give proper thought to a technology that does not immediately seem to fall within their geographic potential. The key to using CSP in Europe would be a HVDC direct current grid. There exists a German-financed scenario, showing how all of Europe's renewable energies could be linked to such a grid, doing wonders for the solidarity of Europe in the face of threats to energy security. Perhaps most importantly the case for CSP is squeezed out by louder voices. The countries with most to gain – North Africa, Egypt, Jordan, Iran and India – are not traditionally regarded as players in the energy politics of the European Union. The technical and geo-political case for CSP linked to an HVDC grid, looks to me to be overwhelming. Californian investment in it has risen sharply since 2006. Anyone who cares about the future of our energy and environment policies should be echoing David Cameron and crying, "Let sunshine win the day".

The practice of public affairs is very much in the news this summer. When Nancy Pelosi, the Speaker of the US House of Representatives, introduced the charmingly named "Open Government, Honest Leadership Act", she declared: "With the passage of the Act we draw back the curtains, throw up the windows and let the sunshine in". Elsewhere the House of Commons is currently investigating lobbying, while in Vienna the political world is convulsed by a pair of lobbying-related scandals. This autumn in Brussels will see the next instalment of the complex struggle over the European Transparency Initiative. Both politicians and public affairs practitioners should bear in mind Michael Ignatieff's injunction not to cocoon themselves in the inner world of their own imaginings nor to confuse the world as it is with the world as they wish it to be.

Originally written as an ECPA Briefing, August 2007.

4. *First Things, Last Things: The Public Affairs of Priority*

Tom Spencer

December 13th is not technically mid-winter. However the coincidence of the signing of the Reform Treaty in Lisbon and the joint initiative by 20 Central Banks to address the global liquidity crisis, make it a good day on which to reflect on the setting of priorities and the establishment of coherent policy. The signature in the Jerónimos Monastery marks the completion of the second stage of the European Union's recovery of its confidence. Two years ago the Union was faced with the triple need to sort out its leadership vacuum, to unpick the mess around the Constitution and to agree on a new metaprogramme – a theme that could be communicated to the people of Europe. With the exception of the UK, a new and more confident leadership is in place. The Reform Treaty is both useful and outward looking. The direction of a "Europe in the World" policy has been set. That the Treaty is being signed at the point of departure of the Portuguese discoverers will have escaped no one.

A similar triple exercise is in progress at global level. The leadership of Russia and China for the next ten years is now clear. Whatever the twists and turns of the soap opera, otherwise known as the US Presidential Primaries, the name of the Democrat Party Presidential candidate will be clearer earlier than usual at the start of 2008. The process leading to the signature of a post-Kyoto agreement on climate change can be interfered with by the USA in the dying months of the Bush Administration, but it now looks unlikely to be derailed. The initiative by the 20 Central Banks brings a long overdue recognition that the credit crisis, triggered by sub-prime lunacy, now threatens the real world as well as the job prospects of bankers who danced into the flames in the thrall of groupthink. Avoiding a global recession and correcting global imbalances to reflect the new reality of the global economy is now an immediate priority, rather than a theoretical possibility. In parallel the tangled paralysis of foreign policy at last shows some signs of movement. The prospect of a US attack on Iran has receded. There are even some tentative signposts to a way out of the twin quagmires of Iraq and Afghanistan.

Strangely it seems that it is only in the UK that this sense of a mid-winter turning point cannot be detected. I predicted in August that Gordon Brown would not have the nerve to call a snap election in October, but I had not anticipated the complete paralysis that has affected one of the most intellectual politicians ever to be Prime Minister. To govern is to choose. Deciding what to do first is the everyday duty of a Prime Minister. Gordon Brown should abandon his increasingly embarrassing quest for the "Vision Thing". He does not have the deadly Blair eloquence which allowed the previous Prime Minister for many years to constantly redefine himself as situations changed. The country would have a higher opinion of Mr Brown if it thought him capable of setting priorities and sticking to them. As usual the fault line in British politics shows up on the European issue. Gordon Brown rightly concluded that a referendum on the Treaty would dominate the available time that he had inherited from Tony Blair. It was logical therefore to renege on the foolish promise to conduct a referendum on the issue. However he makes himself look foolish by avoiding Brussels and photo opportunities involving champagne or collective Treaty signing.

By contrast, David Cameron has had a good autumn. His nerve, and that of the Conservative Party, held during the crucial weeks in October. He was on solid ground in calling for a referendum as long as he could be certain that there would not be one. A referendum on Europe would have irretrievably re-opened the wounds in the Conservative Party and negated his attempt to move the Party onward from its obsession with Europe. He now has to avoid an ugly burst of Euroscepticism in the House of Commons during the parliamentary reading of the Treaty. The British electorate do not need to be reminded of how Europe rendered the Conservative Party unfit for government under its three failed leaders. David Cameron has laid down his priorities. He decided what needed to be done first. The last thing he now needs is to be re-impaled on the European issue.

The ECPA Circle in Brussels in December was treated to a fascinating presentation by a leading recruitment expert specialising in public affairs. He spoke to the title, "What Qualities are we Looking for in Senior Public Affairs Appointments?". The speaker began by showing how the public affairs function was becoming increasingly professionalised and gaining recognition from other management functions. He maintained that the day of the amateur public affairs practitioner, relying on charm and a well-stuffed address book, was clearly past. Public affairs professionals were defined as needing specific competences, most notably about the decision-making process and the mind of regulators of all kinds. Success in public affairs was increasingly being measured against concrete results. In these circumstances choosing your battles wisely, gaining internal and external alignment and leveraging key executives were indicated as important competences. The ability to make complex issues simple for both internal and external audiences was underlined, provided it was allied with the ability to master technical expertise on specific issues. A terrifying list of adjectives describing the ideal public affairs personality followed. The practitioner should be "thorough, investigative, curious, open minded, forward looking and constructive". The successful public affairs personality should be "outgoing, interested in people, capable of listening, focused, tenacious, consensus-driven and communicative". This figure should be both a team player and a team leader, and, just for the hell of it, should be smart and a good linguist! I don't dissent from any of this, but I suspect that the key public affairs skill at senior level is the ability to set priorities and stick to them. My dictionary defines priority as "something given or meriting attention before competing alternatives". Today's public affairs practitioners – whether in-house or consultants, diplomats or trade association executives – live in a world of intense time pressure. I know of no other function where the "urgent" is more likely to drive out the "important". All too often we settle for what can be delivered in the available time, rather than what could be delivered if we followed the Decision Mapping© discipline of scanning the whole external environment of our customer.

Decision influencers push their case too often by resort to volleys of superlatives. Their preferred answer is always "cheapest, quickest or wisest". A few weeks ago a colleague in Brussels observed that the European Centre for Public Affairs was the oldest organisation in Europe devoted to the study of public affairs. We started teaching in 1986, but were not formally established until 22nd April 1988. I was minded to ask if there is an advantage to being the oldest? We were set up to "record, analyse and improve the conduct of public affairs". Surely the true virtue should be in how close we have come to achieving those goals, rather than in how long we have been in existence? St Pancras International, in its much-hyped launch, boasts that it has "the longest champagne bar in Europe". Surely a relevant boast should be about the quality of the champagne and the speed of service rather than its geographic extent?

Of all these dangerous superlatives, the most puzzling and potent are that ancient couple "First" and "Last". I have long thought of assembling a group of public affairs practitioners from companies who are cursed by working for the "leader" in their sector. Such companies acquire perceived responsibilities, which in public affairs terms at least, often more than outweigh the market advantage of their size. Rather like eldest children, they are expected to be better behaved, more organised and more responsible than their junior siblings. Psychologists tell us that place in family has more impact on personality and life chances than any other single factor. Apparently eldest children often marry "spoilt" youngest children in order to cheer themselves up at bit. The Spencer household, on the other hand, is a union of two oldest offspring. It occurs to me that we might commission some research to see what position in family produces the most successful public affairs practitioner.

I am glad that public affairs has increasingly adopted the habit of the advertising industry in establishing annual celebrations of the "Best This or Best That". This is a kind of celebratory benchmarking that should over time lead to the spreading of best practice. I am not sure however that I can find it in myself to welcome the "Worst EU Lobby Award" organised by the opponents of public affairs practice. Judgement by one's peers seems to me a legitimate exercise. Judgement by a random and unlimited audience, without due process, strikes me as questionable.

Eschatology, the study of "Last Things", is a branch of theology, currently somewhat out of fashion. Of course it should not be confused with the study Eshatology which is the interpretation of prophesy! (Thank you Google). Karen Armstrong's latest book is entitled, *The Bible – The Biography*. Amongst many other gems, she points out that it was only in the 19th Century that people began to take the Bible literally. Before that date they valued the stories as myth that made sense of the complexity of human existence. Never for a moment did they believe that God created the world in six days. So much for the credentials of modern day fundamentalists who want to influence American foreign policy on the basis of the Book of Revelation. She also points out that the doctrine of original sin was conceived by St Augustine as a response to the collapse of the Western Roman Empire in his lifetime. What shifts in mankind's thinking can we anticipate as American and European empires give way to Asian power?

Perhaps we would have a better sense of priority if we were more prepared to evaluate our lives and deaths in Tibetan Buddhist style, and to assess the total contribution which we individually make to humanity. Such thoughts are brought to mind by the increasing number of friends who seem determined to disrupt my network by either dying or retiring. Worthwhile public affairs leaves an imprint for better or worse on our collective future. *Ars longa, vita brevis.* Public affairs life is indeed short, even as its impact can be long. We can all improve our effectiveness by being more conscious about how we set our day to day priorities. The ultimate effectiveness may however be in consciously deciding what impact we want to make with our own lives. With the reputation of public affairs increasingly under scrutiny in the democracies, we should all give priority to defending the validity of the common enterprise in which we are engaged. It is comforting that other management functions are increasingly valuing the contribution of good public affairs. However it would be a self-defeating tragedy if the reputation of public affairs practitioners rose inside their own organisations in direct response to the decay in the reputation of public affairs itself. The first thing for all public affairs practitioners to do in 2008 is to concentrate on defending the validity of public affairs in democratic systems. Here as elsewhere in our complicated world Europe can take a lead.

Originally written as an ECPA Briefing, December 2007.

The Future of Public Trust

5. Beyond Black & White – The Public Affairs of Global Crises

Tom Spencer

Most public affairs people know how to cope with a crisis. They have the knowledge, contacts and experience to predict change in a policy sector with a high degree of confidence. They make their living by influencing the outcome of change. It gets more interesting when the need is to understand the interaction of different sectors in crisis. The Institute for Environmental Security explored this dangerous territory in early September with a seminar in Brussels entitled "The Perfect Storm: Trade, Finance & Climate in 2009". It started off as an examination of the climate-friendly changes in the World Trade Organisation, the World Bank and the International Monetary Fund needed to underpin any agreement at the Copenhagen Conference of the Parties on Climate Change. It rapidly became an analysis of the short term inter-connections of the collapse of the Doha Round, the drying up of global credit and the extra problems this presented for climate change negotiations. In the last two weeks of September the various crises, political as well as financial, have merged to produce the potential for systemic change.

Lobbyists have been playing their proper democratic role as carriers of messages between electors and elected. At times however one has the sense that lobbyists have no greater sense of what is likely to flow from their actions than do politicians. The vote on the rescue package in the House of Representatives on Monday 29th September has since been reversed, but it nonetheless stands as a classic of political miscommunication. The next few years will either make or break the existing political structures of the planet as we struggle to understand the interaction of foreign policy, financial stability, economic interaction, trade and climate change. None of these crises are best handled by the black and white simplicity of political slogans. I rather like the idea, aired recently in the UK, of a campaign to print t-shirts with the slogan, "I think you'll find it's a bit more complicated than that". Campaigners thus dressed would be invited to stand next to those wearing t-shirts with simple slogans like "Ban the Bomb" or "Make Poverty History".

Ever since mankind started to burn fossil fuel we have emitted Black Carbon into the atmosphere. We used to call it soot. I am just old enough to remember when London was permanently black and prone to terrible smogs. The developed world cleaned up its Black Carbon emissions in the 1960s. For much of Asia however the emission of soot continues. It settles on the snow and ice of the planet. Its blackness reduces by 40% the reflective whiteness of the cryosphere – the world of ice and snow. This is known as the albedo effect. It has been studied in the Arctic for some time. Only recently has it become apparent that the damage is likely to be more extreme in the Himalayas. The industrial sites of Asia are not as heavily regulated as those of Europe. Forests are still burnt on a regular basis. In India 70% of domestic cooking and heating uses firewood as its fuel. The latest evidence from the Potsdam Institute for Climate Impact Research predicts catastrophic melting of the Himalayan glaciers in the 2020s. With such melting goes the summer water supply for all the great rivers of Asia. It should be an open and shut case for immediate action. Clean up marine fuel, cut down on diesel usage, put simple technology in place to capture the soot at source on Asian industrial plants. More action to inhibit the burning of tropical forests would help. Getting the Indian rural poor to switch to stoves burning on the pyrolysis principle, producing Biochar that can be used as a soil enhancer and ready made carbon store, would be even more helpful. One might think that Black Carbon and snow was a black and white issue. One would be wrong. Because Black Carbon is not a gas, its reduction is not being negotiated in the UNFCCC Copenhagen process. A classic example of people in one silo not communicating with those in another! Yet for those who want to find a way of moving India and China towards a deal, Black Carbon should be central as the great game of finding a global deal on the climate inches forward with the speed of continental drift.

Some years have the sense of the tectonic plates of humanity shifting beneath our feet. The Czechoslovaks were rightfully suspicious of any year with an 8 at the end: the foundation of the Republic in 1918, the Munich Agreement in 1938, the Communist coup in 1948 and the Russian invasion in 1968. The 40th anniversary of 1968 has been marked on the BBC by five minute programmes of radio clips reproducing the day-by-day atmosphere of those "revolutionary times". I was twenty in 1968. My time was spent struggling against the Marxist domination of my university and most of those across Europe. When not struggling with the far Left, I was inspired by pan-European dreams of what we would later come to know as a "Europe – Whole and Free". The Warsaw Pact invasion of Czechoslovakia was a life changing experience. It destroyed the credibility of the New Left as well as the old. It underlined the stark reality of a continent divided by

Russian aggression. When you are 20, everything is seen in vivid colours. I remember taking the Luscher Colour Test in 1969 and discovering that my favourite colours were black and red, indicative of a love of drama, clarity and division. However no sooner had the book revealed this aspect of my personality, than it also revealed that this was the logic of Hitler's choice of colours for his reversal of the Swastika. But then these were revolutionary times. To be young was indeed very heaven. Rhetoric without bounds, travel without limit and sex without AIDS. We held views about Us and Them, good and evil, capitalism and communism. It was all very open and shut, very black and white. All the world was dualist, simple and predictable. We thought we understood about black swans and white swans. Nowadays the survivors of 1968 are not so sure. Our hair, our suits and our beliefs have all gone grey.

The book which is most relevant for current global crises is *The Black Swan: The Impact of the Highly Improbable*, by Nassim Taleb. He defines a whole category of events which he calls "black swans". These are important events which change human behaviour massively, which were not anticipated, but which can be eloquently explained after the event. The internet is a black swan, just as are CNN or 9/11. Taleb points to the weakness of the Bell Curve as a predictor of human behaviour. It is events at the extremes which bring about real change, but which in most scientific and political analysis are dismissed as too unlikely to be relevant. It is the philosophy of the Bell Curve that leads to "group think" and the perpetuation of obviously doomed behaviour. The crisis gripping the financial world today was easily predictable as the consequence of lax regulation and of greed within a flawed structure of reward. As with all bubbles it is amazing that so many people could believe in the sustainability of the unsustainable. Sir John Templeton, who died in August, practised the lessons of the Black Swan 30 years before its publication. He presented Templeton College, Oxford with a handsome sum of money while I was Associate Dean there in the mid-1980s. He spoke like a slowed down version of the *Reader's Digest*, but he understood one major source of wisdom. He refused to be swept away by the momentum of the herd. He took the decisions which made him one of the world's most successful global investors at his house in the Bahamas, rather than amidst the excitements of Wall Street. Issues for him had time dimensions. He famously bought nuclear shares in the days after Three Mile Island. They were not black and white; they were exquisitely wrought grey insights. History is a good corrective for the traps in the Bell Curve. Alexander Hoare, who is the current Managing Partner of C Hoare & Co., the bank founded in 1672, tells the story of how his father educated him about banking by showing him the internal records of the Bank during the South Sea Bubble of 1720! The global crises of autumn 2008 form a classic Black Swan. They will change all our lives. They were not anticipated, but there is now a whole industry eloquently explaining them *ex post facto*.

The idea of Europe has undergone its own seismic shifts in the last 40 years. In 1968 the European Economic Community was an unchallenged success, but it was still five years away from admitting its first new members. Nobody thought to continually pick it up by its roots and vote on it. Since 1999 the European Union has been pursuing a black and white idea in a grey world. After the shambles of the Santer resignation, the institutions of the Union, led by the Commission, set out on a crusade for transparency and communication. They believed that if only they could explain the European Union to the electorates of Europe, all would be well. They tried campaigns in primary schools. They tried communications packages. They tried new treaties. Then they tried new ways of having new treaties involving ever more people. Eventually a Constitution emerged from a Convention. The French and Dutch electorates said No, albeit for reasons unrelated to the text. So the governments tried again with the Treaty of Lisbon and this time the Irish said No. I increasingly come to believe that we need to recognise that the electorates of Europe are not that interested in what their political classes do in the corridors of Brussels. We should abandon the attempt to change the Treaties, with all the accompanying opportunities for Eurosceptic excitement. We should instead do as much as possible without treaty change, using Inter-Institutional Agreements wherever possible. Cherry picking is the wrong word for this process. The situation is as follows. The mandate for change delivered by 27 governments and the European Parliament is deemed insufficient. It has proved impossible to communicate the complexity of the European Union to electorates. The whole process has become a blood sport for populists. Europe's political classes should stop this demeaning dance and decide what needs to be done in the interests of a small continent in a troubled world. Within these constraints, nothing very radical will be achieved, but at least political energies will be directed towards real policies rather than political theatre.

My pessimism on this subject stems from the fact that I don't believe that the Irish electorate can be expected to vote again on the text of the Treaty of Lisbon. The only clue they gave us for rejection in June was the loss of the future certainty of an Irish Commissioner when the size of the Commission was reduced from 27 to 20 in 2014. The question of the month amongst Euro-nerds is speculation that, in the absence of the Treaty of Lisbon, the Treaty of Nice would apply with its automatic reduction of the number of Commissioners to 20 in 2009! Great! So what's to change? Historians will decide why the Irish Referendum on Lisbon was lost. At the moment the favoured explanation is the extraordinary smug short sightedness of the Irish political elite. I prefer a greyer explanation involving the amount of US Neo-Conservative money backing the "Libertas" campaign. For those seeking details much can be found in the Irish press. Much more will be discovered as the accounts of the referendum are explored by MEPs trying to track down the truth about the missing 1.3 million euros. It would not be elegant for an Englishman to speculate on the feeling of an Irish electorate, were it to discover that it had been subverted by dirty American money. It would not be the first time that certain Americans have decided that a weakened Europe was in America's interest. Russia's adventures in Georgia should be enough to warn us against such competitive short sightedness across the Atlantic. Indeed there is some evidence of Neo-Conservative meddling at both the Eastern and Western extremities of Europe. I gather that President Sarkozy made it clear on his visit to Tbilisi that he had come to see the President of Georgia, not a bevy of Neo-Conservative advisors, fresh in from life as staffers in Washington.

One of the saddest losses of the summer was the death, in a car crash, of Bronislaw Geremek, MEP and former Foreign Minister of Poland. Of all the great and the good who appeared before the European Parliament's Foreign Affairs Committee under my chairmanship in the late 1990s, he was the only one who received a standing ovation. In 20 minutes Geremek re-educated the Committee. He communicated a Polish world view as only a medieval historian could. In retrospect it's a tragedy that a man of such courage and intellect was denied the Presidency of the European Parliament. Much ink is being spilled about the Russian attack on Georgia, not least because it came almost on the anniversary of the invasion of Czechoslovakia. I hold probably heretical views on this subject. It seems to me that both Europe and America have drawn the wrong conclusions from the success of EU Enlargement to date. Blinded by the belief that Turkey would join the European Union, the powers that be have assumed that the Black Sea can be turned into a European lake as a way of "containing" Russia. The likelihood of Turkish membership is now so infinitely remote as to be unwise as the basis for any policy, let alone something as significant as our relationship with Russia.

Why have we chosen to endow the borders inherited from the internal administration of the Soviet Union with all the sanctity of ancient nation states? This is nonsense. The Crimea was never historically part of the Ukraine. As Geremek knew, Eastern Ukraine itself never experienced the medieval links to Poland-Lithuania that would make the Western Ukraine a coherent part of the European Union. It would have been wrong to deny Kosovo independence because of the internal boundary design of a defunct Yugoslavia. I see no reason why we should worry too much about the "loss" of South Ossetia or Abkhazia. We need a major "realist" re-think of European interests in the Black Sea. The starting point for such a review should be that the political and economic coherence of the Union must not be sacrificed on the altar of simplistic geo-politics. We have an interest in helping the Georgians and Armenians strengthen their links with Europe. We have an interest in reducing Russia's ability to exert energy blackmail towards Europe. We do not help either ourselves or the Georgians by making rhetorical promises which we are unable to keep. A Western Ukraine would fit easily inside the European Union, with its own language and powerful national memories. It would make a much greater contribution to European security than attempting to dragoon all of the Ukraine into both NATO and the EU. Europeans should remember that we have been here before. If one visits Novorossiysk they point to the spot where the White Russian Black Sea Fleet was scuttled at the end of the Russian Civil War.

The American Presidential campaign has been compulsive watching for Europeans for the last 12 months. The prospect of an Obama Presidency is intensely exciting for Europeans. Not only would it mark a complete break with the current Administration, more importantly it would allow Europeans to feel comfortable about liking America once again. The spectacle of a bi-racial candidate ascending to the highest office in what is still the world's most powerful nation is irresistible soap opera. The fact that he embodies everything that Europe would like to think about itself in terms of intellect, sophistication and balance is icing on the cake.

I do not know whether Obama or McCain will win in November. The only thing which could stop Obama is a question of black and white. In all the fuss over an exceptional man, I believe that more attention should have been paid to the difficulties of being a black American voter rather than a black American candidate. The traditional efforts to restrict Afro-American registration are taking new forms. "Strong forces are at work to downsize the electorate, ostensibly to combat fraud and strip the rolls of voters who are ineligible for one reason or another. But the real effect is to make it harder for many black Americans to vote, largely because they are more vulnerable to challenges than other parts of the population"[1]. For example, recent moves in some States require photo ID before voter registration is permitted. For most Americans this means driving licences. Driving licences are least commonly held by black Americans in inner city areas. It remains amazing to European eyes that 17 States deny voting rights to those who have completed their prison sentences. In many States the voting list is kept up to date by computer programmes, searching for ineligible voters. In Florida for example, it only requires that 80% of the letters in your name match with the name of someone with a criminal record. Black men and women are six times more likely to be in prison than whites, so it is not surprising that these methods result in the further reduction of Afro-American participation.

It is common currency that Obama will face the problem of the so called "Bradley gap". This maintains that 7% of the white population, who say they will vote for black candidates, decline to do so in the privacy of the voting booth. Several States are holding ballots to ban affirmative action thus putting the issue of white resentment into voters' minds. Obama needs to court as many white voters as possible if he is to counter these in-built disadvantages.

My instinct is that Obama will win by a small majority, with the breakthrough coming in the Mountain States. For a time it looked as though the choice of Sarah Palin as Vice Presidential candidate was going to usher in a re-run of the "culture wars". A wise American of my acquaintance maintains that Obama/Biden will win because McCain/Palin will make more mistakes. I believe that elections in hard times are determined by more fundamental issues. "It's the Economy, Stupid" is given massively extra force by the rolling collapse in American financial

---

1. Hacker, A. (2008) "Obama: The Price of Being Black," *New York Review of Books*, 25 September.

institutions. It would seem that this year's "October surprise" has come early, with the financial melt-down coming to dominate the closing weeks of the election. This takes us back to the tension between wise government and populism which is underlined during global crises of all kinds. The populist treatment of Trade is not in America's economic interest. The reluctance to pay higher petrol prices inhibits sensible American policy on climate change. The interpretation of the rise in the price of oil as an energy security issue has given the coal lobbies a major opportunity, while leaving solar power without government subsidy. The voting figures on the rejection of the Paulson Deal tell the story of politicians of both parties bowing to public prejudice. The truth is that such populism has a real price in governmental credibility. A Vice President who believed in Creationism may be seen by some Americans as a charming assertion of America's right to idiosyncrasy. To the rest of the world it looks like a political system that is losing its grip. In such times both lobbyists and politicians need to consider the impact of all their actions. Everything is connected to everything else. The unexpected does happen. Radical shifts do occur. Paradoxically Obama and his call for change could be a more certain way of preserving the essentials of America's reputation and the current economic and political system than the global spasm likely to be engendered by Republican market fundamentalism. Of course I could be wrong, in which case please don your t-shirt with the slogan "I think you'll find it's a bit more complicated than that".

Originally written as an ECPA Briefing, September 2008.

Part IV. AUTHORS' BIOGRAPHIES

Dr. Steven Billet is the Director of the Master's in Legislative Affairs in the Graduate School of Political Management, The George Washington University. Before joining the faculty at GWU, he worked as an advocate in the AT&T family of companies for 18 years. This included six years as the Director of Government Relations for Europe, Africa and the Middle East.

Michael Burrell is Edelman's Vice Chairman, Europe. His responsibilities include oversight of all the firm's European public affairs businesses. Based in London, he works particularly closely with the London and Brussels public affairs teams. Prior to joining Edelman in 2002, Michael was Chairman of Westminster Strategy, a leading London public affairs consultancy, and of Grayling Political Strategy, its Brussels sister operation. He founded Westminster Strategy in 1986. From 2000 to 2002 he was chairman of the Association of Professional Political Consultants, the self-regulatory body for the UK's public affairs industry. Michael is a Deputy Chairman of the European Centre for Public Affairs. *PR Week* named Michael as one of the 100 most influential industry figures in its 21-year history, and *Public Affairs* News has described him as a "European public affairs legend". He is the author of *Lobbying and the Media: Working with Politicians and Journalists*. Before becoming a consultant, Michael was a political correspondent, reporting on both UK and European politics. He was educated at St Peter's College, Oxford, where he read Philosophy, Politics and Economics.

P. Nikiforos Diamandouros is, as of 1 April 2003, the European Ombudsman. From 1998 to 2003, he was the first National Ombudsman of Greece. He has also been Professor of Comparative Politics at the Department of Political Science and Public Administration of the University of Athens since 1993 (currently on leave). Mr Diamandouros has written extensively on the politics and history of Greece, Southern Europe and Southeastern Europe and, more specifically, on democratisation, state and nation-building, and the relationship between culture and politics. He received his B.A. degree from Indiana University (1963) and his M.A. (1965), M.Phil. (1969) and Ph.D. (1972) degrees from Columbia University.

Dr. Ingo Friedrich is Quaestor and Member of the Bureau of the European Parliament since 2007. He has been a Member of the EU Parliament since 1979 when the first direct elections took place. From 1999 until 2007, he was Vice-President of the institution. Since 1993, he is Vice-President of his party, the Christian Social Union (CSU) of Germany. He also gives lectures in "European Business" at the University of Applied Sciences in Ansbach, Germany.

Erik Jonnaert graduated from Gent Law School and holds degrees from Harvard and Texas Universities. He joined Procter and Gamble in 1985, holding a succession of legal, public affairs and government relations posts, culminating in his appointment as Vice President External Relations Asia in 2007. He is a past chair of the Management Board of the ECPA, is a member of the board of the Chamber of Commerce Halle-Vilvoorde, the American Chamber of Commerce Belgium and the Flemish Employers Federation. He is Chairman of the UNICE European Consumer Products Coordination Group and the UNICE Consumer Affairs and Marketing Committee, as well as being a member of the advisory and support board for the Union of European Employers Federation.

Dr. Peter Köppl is managing partner of Kovar & Köppl Public Affairs Consulting, based in Vienna, Austria's leading consultancy focusing on political management and political communications. His PhD on Lobbying the European Union was awarded by the University of Vienna, and he also holds a Master of Arts in Political Management from the Graduate School of Political Management (GSPM), George Washington University in Washington, D.C. He is Senior Research Fellow at DIPA (German Institute for Public Affairs; Berlin), co-founder of ALPAC (Austrian Lobbying & Public Affairs Council), and a member of the ECPA's management board. Previously he was in charge of Government Relations and Media Relations at the Austrian Federal Medical Association, and held positions as Senior Vice President with the Austrian affiliates of Burson-Marsteller and Weber-Shandwick. He started his career as assistant to the Secretary General of the Austrian Federal Board for Industry and Environmental Relations and later on he worked in the department for Corporate Communications of a large Austrian multinational industry group. Peter Koeppl is author of various books, teaches at several universities and is a frequent speaker on Public Affairs and Lobbying in the German speaking market.

Authors' Biographies

José Lalloum is a founder and managing partner of LOGOS Public Affairs, with special responsibility for environmental and health issues. A European public affairs and communication specialist of French nationality, he has been active in Brussels since 1991 as a consultant, director of public affairs consultancies, and Secretary General of a European Federation. José has advised a large number of multinational companies, European federations, and French and British organisations on their public affairs strategies and activities. He has conducted lobbying campaigns in a wide range of fields, including health, trade, consumer policy, the environment, and taxation. A trained facilitator, he is founder and President of the European Centre for Complex Issue Resolution (ECCIR). Prior to working in Brussels, he worked in Paris in trade and public affairs. He has a degree in Marketing, Communications and Linguistics, and a post-graduate degree in European Law from the Jean Monnet Faculty of Law (Paris XI). José was elected Chairman of EPACA, the European Public Affairs Consultancies' Association, in March 2007 for a two-year term.

Dr. Conor McGrath is an Independent Scholar, and Deputy Editor of the *Journal of Public Affairs*. He was Lecturer in Political Lobbying and Public Affairs at the University of Ulster in Northern Ireland from 1999 to 2006. Before becoming an academic, he worked for a Conservative Member of Parliament in the UK and for a Republican Congressman, as Public Affairs Director at a public relations company, and as a self-employed lobbyist. His books include *Lobbying in Washington, London and Brussels: The Persuasive Communication of Political Issues* (2005), *Challenge and Response: Essays on Public Affairs and Transparency* (2006, co-edited with Tom Spencer), and *Irish Political Studies Reader: Key Contributions* (2008, co-edited with Eoin O'Malley). He is currently editing a three-volume collection on *Interest Groups & Lobbying*, to be published in 2009. He served as president of the Political Studies Association of Ireland from 2005 to 2007.

Dr. Irina Michalowitz is the EU Representative of the Austria-based mobile network operator "mobilkom austria group". She is a political scientist specialising in European integration studies. Prior to joining mobilkom austria group, she worked as the Research Policy Project Manager of the European Platform of Women Scientists (EPWS), Brussels, responsible for policy analysis and interest representation, and she was Assistant Professor in the Department of Political Science at the Institute for Advanced Studies in Vienna, Austria. Before that, she worked in the Public Affairs Division of Preussag AG in Bonn and Brussels and, as a member of the European Doctoral College, completed a joint German-French doctoral thesis on the topic of EU lobbying strategies at the Universities of Hamburg and Strasburg. She also teaches at the United Business Institutes, Brussels and at the Donau University Krems, Austria. She has published two monographs and various peer-reviewed international journal articles, among them *EU-Lobbying – Principals, Agents and Targets. Strategic Interest Intermediation in EU Policy-Making* (2004; Münster: LIT); *Lobbying in der EU* (2007; Vienna: WUV/UTB), and "What Determines Influence? Assessing Conditions for Decision-Making Influence of Interest Groups in the EU" (*Journal of European Public Policy*, 14(1), pp. 132-151).

Jens Nymand Christensen is Director for Institutional Affairs and Better Regulation in the Secretariat General of the European Commission. He studied economics at the University of Washington, and holds an MBA from Copenhagen Graduate School of Economics and Business Administration. Mr Nymand Christensen served as an advisor on economic and trade issues to the ALDE group of the European Parliament from 1979 to 1984. He was a member of the Cabinet of Henning Christophersen, Vice President of the European Commission 1985-1993. He then worked as Head of the Representation in Denmark of the European Commission 1993-1997, and as Head of Unit for Consumer Affairs 1997-2000. From 2000 to 2002, he was Head of Unit for International Food Safety, and then Head of Office of Henning Christophersen at the Convention drafting the new Treaty from 2002 to 2003. He has been a Director at the Secretariat General since 2003.

Amber Price started her career working in European Union legal research at Freshfields Bruckhaus Deringer in Brussels and went on to begin her public affairs career with the European paper industry. Having joined Nike in 2004, she now works in European Union and Member State Government and Public Affairs, managing a broad range of policy areas. She has recently been appointed General Secretary of ECPA II, a daughter organisation of ECPA. Amber has a BA in Classical Studies and French from the University of Exeter and is a recent graduate of the University of Stirling where she received a Master of Science in Public Relations in 2008. Her research interests focus predominantly on new Social Media and the changing face of Public Affairs.

Authors' Biographies

Kristian Schmidt is Deputy Head of Cabinet for Vice-President Siim Kallas, Vice-President of the European Commission. He was previously Deputy Head of Cabinet for Commissioner Poul Nielson (Development and Humanitarian Aid), and before that a career diplomat in the Danish foreign service, serving at Denmark's Permanent Mission to the UN in New York. He is trained in economics, political science and international relations, and holds university degrees and diplomas from the University of Cambridge (UK), the University of Copenhagen, (Denmark), Sciences Politiques, Paris (F), Università di Bologna (It) and Aix (F).

Tom Spencer is Executive Director of the European Centre for Public Affairs and Visiting Professor of Public Affairs at Brunel University, Uxbridge. He worked for Peat Marwick Mitchell & Co and was then Assistant to the Director of the "Britain in Europe" Referendum Campaign in 1975. He worked in the United States Senate and then joined J Walter Thompson & Co where he was responsible for the Guinness advertising. He was Associate Dean of Templeton College, Oxford from 1984-1989. A Member of the European Parliament for Derbyshire from 1979 to 1984 and for Surrey from 1989 – 1999, he was Chairman of the Conservatives in the European Parliament 1994-97. From 1997-99 he was President of the European Parliament's Committee on Foreign Affairs, Human Rights and Defence Policy. As a committed environmentalist he was, from 1995-99, President of GLOBE International (Global Legislators Organisation for a Balanced Environment) He was Chairman of Counterpart Europe (2000-2002) an NGO active in 60 countries. He was a Commissioner of the Commission on Globalisation (2000-2003). He was Visiting Professor of Global Governance at the University of Surrey (2000-2004). He is Vice Chairman to the Institute for Environmental Security in the Hague, a Director of Action for a Global Climate Community, and a member of the Conservative Party's Quality of Life Group on Climate Change since 2006. His e-mail address is tom@tomspencer.info, his website is www.tomspencer.info.

Roland Verstappen is Vice President, International Affairs, Arcelor Mittal. He became Chairman of the ECPA Management Board in June 2008. Before 2006 he was Executive Director, European Governmental Affairs for the Ford Motor Company. In this role, he was responsible for all governmental policy issues for Ford, Jaguar, Land Rover, Volvo and

Mazda. He was appointed to this position in 2000. Previously, he has held several other positions in Ford starting as in-house legal counsel in Ford Belgium in 1985. In 1988, he was transferred to the European legal office to handle European mergers, acquisitions, joint ventures, etc. From 1993 to 1995 he was responsible for European affairs in the European office of Ford in Brussels. From 1995 to 2000, he was Director of Governmental Affairs for Ford.